I0160733

# KING OF THE NORTH

### BY
### HEIDI HEIKS

**TEACH Services, Inc.**
P U B L I S H I N G
*www.TEACHServices.com*

World rights reserved. This book or any portion thereof may not be copied or reproduced in any form or manner whatever, except as provided by law, without the written permission of the publisher, except by a reviewer who may quote brief passages in a review. The author assumes full responsibility for the accuracy of all facts and quotations as cited in this book.

This book was written to provide accurate and authoritative information in regard to the subject matter covered. It is sold with the understanding that the publisher is not engaged in giving legal, accounting, medical or other professional advice. If legal advice or other professional expert assistance is required, the reader should seek a competent professional person.

Copyright © 2009 Heidi Heiks and TEACH Services, Inc.
ISBN-13: 978-1-57258-603-1
ISBN-10: 1-57258-603-6
Library of Congress Control Number: 2009929404

Published by

**TEACH Services, Inc.**
P U B L I S H I N G
*www.TEACHServices.com*

# DEDICATION

May this exposition faithfully serve the Seventh-day
Adventist Church as a light unto her path and
guide the 11th hour workers who will hear
the final call of the Bridgegroom to
finish the work to completion,
is my sincere prayer.

Heidi Heiks

# FOREWORD

There are two schools of thought on the interpretation of Daniel 11, especially the closing verses which are seen as still to be fulfilled in the future. The first may be called the literal historical view in which the kings of the north and south are seen as literal geo-political entities in the present day Middle East. Adventist interpreters favored this view until the end of World War I when the British and the Turks fought a battle at Megiddo (Armageddon), but Christ did not come after it.

This failure led to the development of the second view, what may be called the spiritual or symbolic interpretation.

By the end of World War II most Adventist interpreters had adopted this view. In this case the king of the south no longer refers to Egypt but it is seen as a symbol for an end time spiritual or political power. Likewise the king of the north is no longer Syria, but an alternate opposing spiritual or political power. In this school of thought search is made for a fitting application for these symbols and several possibilities need to be considered. Brother Heiks stands squarely within the parameters of the symbolic approach and he has given careful and detailed consideration to the possibilities that need to be examined in carrying out his search for the correct application of these symbols.

> William H. Shea, Ph.D.
> Retired Professor: Old Testament Department
> Seminary, Andrews University
> Retired Associate: Biblical Research Institute
> General Conference of Seventh-day Adventists

* * * * * * *

iv

# PREFACE

Daniel 11:40-12:1 has been difficult exegetical ground for a long time but sound hermeneutical principles guide in the end-time interpretation of the events of Daniel. Accompanied by historical, Biblical, or Spirit of Prophecy explanations, should suffice not only to illuminate divine prophecy in Daniel as it relates to closing events of earthly history, but also to strengthen our faith in a God who "declares the end from the beginning, and from ancient times the things that are not yet done." Isa. 46:9-10. With a solid understanding, we can then go forth to teach and preach the prophetic truth with conviction and in love to a dying world.

> "All heaven is looking upon you who claim to believe the most sacred truth ever committed to mortals. Angels are waiting with longing desire to cooperate with you in working for the salvation of souls." Ellen White, *Selected Messages*, 2:136.

Let us commence, then, in humility as we tread lightly on unfulfilled prophecy, that this exposition may rightly present to the reader the intent and purpose Heaven so desired to convey in warning the church of the obstacles she must meet and the degree of faith that will be required of all to be able to stand when Michael Himself shall stand up. We must fortify our minds with the truth and this truth must produce a faith in each of us that will become a living personal experience. Thus, that we press ever onward for that united faith that in turn will bring forth a united front is my sincere prayer. All emphasis is mine unless otherwise noted, scripture quotations are taken from the KJV.

Heidi Heiks

We begin with the first of the verses under study:

**Dan. 11:40 "And at the time**[6256] **of the end**[7093] **shall the king**[4428] **of the south**[5045] **push**[5055] **at**[5973] **him: and the king**[4428] **of the north**[6828] **shall come against him like a whirlwind,**[8175, 5921] **with chariots,**[7393] **and with horsemen,**[6571] **and with many**[7227] **ships;**[591] **and he shall enter**[935] **into the countries,**[776] **and shall overflow**[7857] **and pass over."**[5674]

One must first identify and understand significant words, phrases and symbols in each verse before one can hope to come to a correct interpretation. Then appropriate time and place for their intended Biblical application can be ascertained.


### DAN. 11:40..."And at the THE TIME OF THE END"...

When is the time of the end? This time period began in 1798. Inspiration has identified it as such in the following:

"The message of salvation has been preached in all ages; but this message is a part of the gospel which could be proclaimed only in the last days, for only then would it be true that the hour of judgment had come. The prophecies present a succession of events leading down to the opening of the judgment. This is especially true of the book of Daniel. But that part of his prophecy which related to the last days, Daniel was bidden to close up and seal 'to the time of the end.' Not till we reach this time could a message concerning the judgment be proclaimed, based on the fulfillment of these prophecies. But at the time of the end, says the prophet, 'many shall run to and fro, and knowledge shall be increased.' Daniel 12:4.

"The apostle Paul warned the church not to look for the coming of Christ in his day. 'That day shall not come,' he says, 'except there come a falling away first, and that man of sin be revealed.' 2 Thessalonians 2:3. Not till after the great apostasy, and the long period of the reign of the 'man of sin,' can we look for the advent of our Lord. The 'man of sin,' which is also styled 'the mystery of iniquity,' 'the son of perdition,' and 'that wicked,' represents the papacy, which, as foretold in prophecy, was to maintain its supremacy for 1260 years. This period

1

ended in 1798. The coming of Christ could not take place before that time. Paul covers with his caution the whole of the Christian dispensation down to the year 1798. It is this side of that time that the message of Christ's second coming is to be proclaimed.

"No such message has ever been given in past ages. Paul, as we have seen, did not preach it; he pointed his brethren into the then far-distant future for the coming of the Lord. The Reformers did not proclaim it. Martin Luther placed the judgment about three hundred years in the future from his day. But since 1798 the book of Daniel has been unsealed, knowledge of the prophecies has increased, and many have proclaimed the solemn message of the judgment near."[1]

## DAN. 11:40…"shall THE KING OF THE SOUTH"…

The King of the South is the King of Egypt. (See, Daniel 11:5–9). Those who have the fall of Communism in 1989 derived from Dan. 11:40 have to try to make a distinction between the King of the South in verse 40 and the King of Egypt, the "land of Egypt" in verse 42 to uphold their supposition even though they are one and the same entity. This is of private interpretation and a wrestling of the scriptures as we will illustrate. This is done to escape the fact that when the King of the North advances to conquer "Egypt," the "land of Egypt"—the "King of the South" in verse 42 they cannot interpret it as one and the same entity for in so doing you then have the King of the North making war with an already defeated foe, a dead horse if you will. Hence, the needed alteration of the symbol when the scriptures allows for no change whatsoever. Who, then, is designated as the "King of the South" and/or "Egypt," the "land of Egypt" in the time of the end? Inspiration defines it this way:

"Of all nations presented in Bible history, Egypt most boldly denied the existence of the living God and resisted His commands. No monarch ever ventured upon more open and highhanded rebellion against the authority of Heaven than did the king of Egypt. When the message was brought him by Moses, in the name of the Lord, Pharaoh proudly answered: 'Who is Jehovah, that I should hearken unto His voice to let Israel

---

1    Ellen White, *Great Controversy,* 356.

go? I know not Jehovah, and moreover I will not let Israel go.' Exodus 5:2, ARV. *This is atheism,* and *the nation represented by Egypt* would give voice to a similar denial of the claims of the living God and would manifest a like spirit of unbelief and defiance....

"According to the words of the prophet, then, a little before the year 1798 some power of satanic origin and character would rise to make war upon the Bible. And in the land where the testimony of God's two witnesses should thus be silenced, there would be manifest the atheism of the Pharaoh and the licentiousness of Sodom.

"This prophecy has received a most exact and striking fulfillment *in the history of France....*"[2]

Atheistic France did push at the papacy in the French Revolution, commencing in 1789. John refers to this event and enlarges upon it in Revelation 11:2–11. Then through Napoleon, the French army entered Rome on the 10th of February, 1798. On February 15th of the same year, the French administered Rome's deadly wound through legislation and the church was forced to recognize the rights of religious liberty and the papacy received her "judicial punishment" as prophesied in Revelation 13:10 (See Strong's word "sword"[3162] in Revelation 13:10 for its intended meaning. The Bible specifies that the "sword"[3162] in Romans 13:4 is the civil or state power). The Church of Rome was deprived of her civil or state backing, rendering the counterfeit church incapable of persecution. In A.D. 508, with Clovis, the union of church and state was "set up"; the marriage was consummated by the Franks (France) in the new world. In 1798 the union of church and state was torn down; the marriage was annulled by the French again—exactly 1290 years later. (For a documented account of how this took place, as well as the legislative documentation that suppressed religious liberty for 1260 years and more, see my website, www.thesourcehh.org. But organized atheism in France is now gone, so who might be designated as the King of the South after the passing of 1798? (Notice that this power would have a "king" or a "kingdom," meaning it is organized, which is not a characteristic of a philosophical force.) The greatest expression of organized atheism today is Communism.

---

2    Ellen White, *Great Controversy*, 269.

It is recognized that the same principles and the same spirit of atheistic France now find their expression in international Communism. Ever since its rise, Communism has been pushing against the papacy. The papacy's greatest fear for many years has been, and still is, the aims, influence and ambitions of Communism. History has shown that since the turn of the 20th century many of the wars have taken place because of competing influences of Communism and Romanism. Accordingly the terms, "the King of the South" and/or "Egypt" the "land of Egypt" is an all-inclusive symbolic term that encompasses all organized atheistic, polytheistic and/or monotheistic kingdoms that deny the sovereignty of Christ at the time of the end:

> *"This is atheism, and the nation represented by Egypt would give voice to a similar denial* of the *claims of the living God* and would manifest a like spirit of unbelief and defiance..."[3]

> "When the children of Israel were gathered out from among the Egyptians, the Lord said: "For I will pass through *the land of Egypt* this night, and will smite all the first-born in *the land of Egypt*, both man and beast; *and against all the gods of Egypt* will I execute judgment: I am the Lord.".…Any one of the children of the Hebrews who was found in the Egyptian habitations was destroyed...."[4]

How do we justify such an interpretation? The hermeneutical principle is this: The things of God before the cross are always taken in a literal and local sense; after the cross, in a symbolic or spiritual and worldwide sense. An example of this is in the last vision of Daniel, chapters 10–12. When we read in Daniel 10:14 and 11:14, we interpret "thy people" as meaning the literal Jews, and rightly so. But then we come to Daniel 12:1, which is part of the vision of chapter 11, for there is no break in the original text and, in fact, the vision does not contextually conclude till verse 3 of chapter 12. In Daniel 12:1, we interpret "thy people" as the saints of God, born-again Christians, spiritual Israel, the Christian Church at the very end of probationary time.

---

3    Ellen White, *Great Controversy*, 269.

4    Ellen White, *Advocate*, July 1, 1899.

So the great question that naturally would be asked is this: How can we move in our interpretation from literal-local to spiritual-worldwide? Wouldn't such interpretations appear inconsistent or contrived? It is well-known that futurists like many evangelicals and others teach that "thy people" in Daniel 12:1 refers to the literal Jews. On the surface, this literal interpretation seems to be consistent and logical. So why do Seventh-day Adventists differ from that approach?

We restate the hermeneutical principle: Before the cross, we interpret the prophetic symbols literally. After the cross and up to the time of the Second Coming, we interpret the prophetic symbols spiritually. In answer to the question above, we have the divine endorsement for doing so in the writings of Paul. In the book of Romans, written after the cross, Paul explains that a Jew is not someone who is such merely by birth, but a Jew is the person who is circumcised or renewed in heart. This is the born-again Christian. He or she has become a spiritual Jew. The term Jew under this dispensation now has a spiritual, worldwide application, as does the city Jerusalem, which is now interpreted and understood to be the Christian Church.

Also, the prophetic principle is that after the Second Coming, we return to literal time. The thousand-year millennium is literally 1000 years. So it is with Babylon. After the cross, Babylon is no longer understood and confined in a literal, local, geographical location. No, Babylon, like the Jew and Jerusalem, is understood as spiritual, worldwide Babylon. And the same Biblical hermeneutical principle applies to the King of the South as well as to the King of the North. Before the cross: literal, local. After the cross: spiritual, worldwide. After the second coming: literal, local.

### DAN. 11:40..."PUSH at him:"

"Push" or "pushing" describes a military conquest:

> Dan. 8:4 "I saw the ram pushing westward, and northward, and southward; so that no beasts might stand before him, neither was there any that could deliver out of his hand; but he did according to his will, and became great."

**DAN. 11:40..."and THE KING OF THE NORTH"...**

The papacy is the King of the North.

The following corroborative statement is taken from a tract by Louis F. Were:

> "The (General Conference) study group appointed by the Committee on Biblical Study and Research presented their 'Report on the Eleventh Chapter of Daniel, With Particular Reference to Verses 36–39,' in 'The Ministry,' March, 1954. The report states definitively: 'Therefore, from the foregoing, we conclude that verses 36–39 of Daniel 11 accurately set forth in prophetic language the work and history of papal Rome.'
>
> "In *The Great Controversy*, page 50, the Lord's messenger undoubtedly refers to Daniel 11:36, saying: 'This compromise between paganism and Christianity resulted in the development of the "man of sin" foretold in prophecy as opposing and exalting himself above God. That gigantic system of false religion is a masterpiece of Satan's power—a monument of his efforts to seat himself upon the throne to rule the earth according to his will.' Daniel declared that 'the king shall do according to his will'—that is, the king of the north, for 'the king' as shown by the context is 'the king of the north.' The Study group referred to above, in its report concerning the subsequent verses in Daniel 11, says: 'Without doubt the Papacy, if it is the power of Daniel 11:36–39, must also play a part in the historical fulfillment of these verses, for the pronoun "him" in verse 40 must refer to the power brought to view in verses 36–39.'
>
> "Thus 'the king' of verse 36 is undoubtedly 'the king of the north' mentioned in Dan. 11:40–45. By applying v. 36 to the Papacy, Mrs. E.G. White disagreed with Uriah Smith's application of Dan. 11:36 to the French Revolution."[5]

The conclusions above are in harmony with the statements of Ellen White, in that the last entity of Daniel 11 is not Turkey, but the papacy:

---

5     Louis F. Were, *The Truth concerning Mrs. E. G. White, Uriah Smith, and the King of the North*, pg. 4.

"The world is filled with storm and war and variance. Yet under one head—the papal power—the people will unite to oppose God in the person of His witnesses."[6]

"Romanism in the Old World and apostate Protestantism in the New will pursue a similar course toward those who honor all the divine precepts."[7]

When one compares Ezekiel 38:15, II Thessalonians 2:7–8, Revelation 13 and 17, to name just a few, the conclusion is inescapable that, through legislation, Rome recovers from her deadly wound and becomes a central figure in the great controversy at the end of time. Keep in mind that Rome will dominate the Old World and apostate Protestantism the New World.

### DAN. 11:40..."shall come against him like a WHIRLWIND"...

This represents destruction:

Prov. 1:27 "When your fear cometh as desolation, and your destruction cometh as a whirlwind; when distress and anguish cometh upon you...."

Jer. 23:19 "Behold, a whirlwind of the LORD is gone forth in fury, even a grievous whirlwind: it shall fall grievously upon the head of the wicked."

Jer. 25:32 "Thus saith the LORD of hosts, Behold, evil shall go forth from nation to nation, and a great whirlwind shall be raised up from the coasts of the earth."

### DAN. 11:40..."with CHARIOTS and HORSEMEN"...

These represent an army:

Ex. 14:9 "But the Egyptians pursued after them, all the horses and chariots of Pharaoh, and his horsemen, and his army, and overtook them encamping by the sea, beside Pihahiroth, before Baalzephon."

---

6    Ellen White, *Testimonies to the Church*, 7:182.

7    Ellen White, *Great Controversy*, 616.

Ex. 14:26 "And the LORD said unto Moses, Stretch out thine hand over the sea, that the waters may come again upon the Egyptians, upon their chariots, and upon their horsemen."

Ex. 14:28 "And the waters returned, and covered the chariots, and the horsemen, and all the host of Pharaoh that came into the sea after them; there remained not so much as one of them."

## DAN. 11:40…"and with many SHIPS;"

Economy, trade, merchandise, merchants, riches—in other words, monetary matters are here named:

Ps. 107:23 "They that go down to the sea in ships, that do business in great waters…."

Let it be remembered that Revelation complements Daniel. Revelation 18:17 shows us how ships are to be understood in the symbolic sense.

Prov. 31:14 "She is like the merchants' ships; she bringeth her food from afar."

Rev. 18:17 "For in one hour so great riches is come to nought. And every shipmaster, and all the company in ships, and sailors, and as many as trade by sea, stood afar off…."

## DAN. 11:40…"and he shall ENTER"…

The verb "enter" means "to besiege."[935] The reader is asked to temporarily accept this definition until additional terms are defined and the meaning of "enter" is revisited.

## DAN. 11:40…"into the COUNTRIES" …

The Hebrew word *eh'-rets*[776] (countries, plural) is indeed found in the original and belongs in this text. Here is where those who say Communism came to its end in verse 40 meet another unanswerable objection. How can such an interpretation be maintained that Communism (Russia, singular) came to its end in 1989 when the prophecy plainly states that the action in verse 40 demands that many "countries" (plural) are to be overthrown when Rome strikes? Thus the specifications do not line up with the facts. When it is explained how and when "he shall enter," it will then be made plain into what he enters.

## DAN. 11:40..."and shall OVERFLOW AND PASS OVER."

A military invasion is depicted, during which nothing can stand in its way. Complete annihilation is here described:

> Dan. 11:10 "But his sons shall be stirred up, and shall assemble a multitude of great forces: and one shall certainly come, and overflow, and pass through: then shall he return, and be stirred up, even to his fortress."

> Isa. 8:7–9 "Now therefore, behold, the Lord bringeth up upon them the waters of the river, strong and many, even the king of Assyria, and all his glory: and he shall come up over all his channels, and go over all his banks: And he shall pass through Judah; he shall overflow and go over, he shall reach even to the neck; and the stretching out of his wings shall fill the breadth of thy land, O Immanuel. Associate yourselves, O ye people, and ye shall be broken in pieces; and give ear, all ye of far countries: gird yourselves, and ye shall be broken in pieces; gird yourselves, and ye shall be broken in pieces."

Now that we have allowed the Bible and Spirit of Prophecy to interpret itself on these Biblical words and phrases of Daniel 11:40, we may confidently begin to evaluate that verse and apply those interpretations to our times—the time of the end. We have already established and generally we think it is agreed by all that the first part of Daniel 11:40 is interpreted as such: "And at the time of the end [1798] shall the king of the south [atheistic France] push at him [the Papacy]." But it is the remainder of verse 40 that depicts a future offensive movement on the part of the papacy that demands a careful analysis. We repeat the verse here, calling your attention to the actions of the king of the north:

> Dan. 11:40 "And at the time[6256] of the end[7093] shall the king[4428] of the south[5045] push[5055] at[5973] him: and the king[4428] of the north[6828] shall come against him like a whirlwind,[8175, 5921]

**with chariots,[7393] and with horsemen,[6571] and with many[7227] ships;[591] and he shall enter[935] into the countries,[776] and shall overflow[7857] and pass over."[5674]**

Daniel gives us five clues for the interpretation, time and place of the events of the latter part of verse 40. Four of them are in verse 40 itself. In his first clue, Daniel indicates in his conventional way that the remainder of Daniel 11:40 is none other than an overview of the remaining events of chapter 11, to be fulfilled in their chronological order. Daniel's first clue is his technique of overview in Daniel 9:24, which was then immediately followed by time-segment details in verses 25 through 27.

Before we can start with an analysis of the four remaining clues in verse 40, it will be necessary to illustrate the four prophetic steps in Satan's plan against God's people at the end of time that Ellen White saw and recorded. She noted the escalating severity of the methods to be used against them to compel them to forsake their allegiance to Jesus. Ironically, it was the same four steps, in the same chronological order used against the Jews in Nazi Germany. These sequential steps will aid us in making correct chronological placement of the events of Daniel 11:40 and add immensely to our understanding of the final events. Ellen White was given a clear understanding of the coming future events:

> "The events connected with the close of probation and the work of preparation for the time of trouble, are clearly presented. But multitudes have no more understanding of these important truths than if they had never been revealed." [8]

Satan's first coercive device is recorded in *Great Controversy* to be fines, imprisonment, and inducements:

> "As the movement for Sunday enforcement becomes more bold and decided, the law will be invoked against commandment keepers. They will be threatened with fines and imprisonment, and some will be offered positions of influence, and other rewards and advantages, as inducements to renounce their faith."[9]

---

8    Ellen White, *Great Controversy*, 594.

9    Ellen White, *Great Controversy*, 607.

Secondly, Satan will arrange that "they will be forbidden to buy or sell." This introduces the financial aspect by way of the term "ships" in the sequence of events in their chronological order.

Satan's third attempt to separate God's people from Him is that "they shall be put to death." The second and third steps are recorded in *The Desire of Ages*:

> "In the last great conflict of the controversy with Satan those who are loyal to God will see every earthly support cut off. Because they refuse to break His law in obedience to earthly powers, they will be forbidden to buy or sell. It will finally be decreed that they shall be put to death. See, Rev. 13:11–17."[10]

Satan's fourth and last scheme is his final solution:

> "The whole world is to be stirred with enmity against Seventh-day Adventists, because they will not yield homage to the papacy, by honoring Sunday, the institution of this antichristian power. It is the purpose of Satan to cause them to be blotted from the earth, in order that his supremacy of the world may not be disputed."[11]

Until this point, the populace would not have been at liberty to slay God's people because that has been the prerogative of governments only. But now a universal death decree issued by the various rulers of Christendom after the second plague (Rev. 16:3–7) gives the infuriated mobs liberty to slay God's people, (See, Ellen White, *Great Controversy*, 626, 628, 631, 635) ironically at the commencement of the fifth plague. (See, Ellen White, *Great Controversy*, 635–6).

> "The decree which is to go forth against the people of God will be very similar to that issued by Ahasuerus against the Jews in the time of Esther."[12]

However, this last device of Satan fails to reap his desired outcome.

---

10  Ellen White, *Desire of Ages*, 121–2.

11  Ellen White, *Testimonies to Ministers*, 37.

12  Ellen White, *Testimonies to the Church*, 5:450.

Returning now to the topic of future oppressive movements mentioned in the latter part of Daniel 11:40, we will start with an analysis of the four remaining clues provided in verse 40. Of course, in staying with the text, one has the likelihood of the best possible interpretation of the text. Never should one walk away from the text for his or her interpretation unless the text is calling for it.

These four remaining clues will confirm that in Daniel 11:40, he repeats his technique of overview followed by time-segment details, as we have already illustrated from Daniel 9:24, 25–27. The second clue, (the first of the four clues to be found in verse 40) then, is the noun "ships." As verified earlier, "ships" introduced a monetary aspect. Since we have only an introduction and not an interpretation here, we therefore will await the interpretation of Dan 11:43, which will shed needed light on this monetary issue. But since Revelation 13 complements and expands on the book of Daniel, we can find in Revelation 13:16–17 a clear connection to the monetary issue at this time. The forbidding to "buy or sell" takes place after the national Sunday law. "…National apostasy, which will end only in national ruin." Ellen White, *Signs of the Times*, March 22, 1910. This national ruin will make the matter of buying and selling a very serious one, indeed. Given our global economy, it will adversely impact the entire world.

The third clue Daniel has given us in his overview will cement the chronology of this event in its chain of events. That clue is the verb "enter," meaning "to besiege" or "to surround." This brings us to two fundamental questions: When does Rome begin her transparent spiritual military conquest for world dominion again, and what precipitates it? The answer is given immediately in Daniel 11:41. We will fully illustrate this premise when we begin our analysis of verse 41.

Daniel's fourth clue for us is the plural noun "countries." Since the Bible is to be read for its most obvious meaning and "countries" carries no symbolic imagery here, Daniel's use of "countries" shows there will be a simultaneous assault, particularly on the countries in the Old World, on the part of Rome. John further reveals that every country in the world will come under the umbrella of the papacy when she begins her military campaign as illustrated in the Revelators overview:

"All the world wondered after the beast." Rev. 13:3.

The fifth and last clue to be found within verse 40 is the compound verb phrase "and shall overflow and pass over." As we have already illustrated, this is a description of total victory. Nothing can stand in Rome's way; complete annihilation is hereby described. Where in Daniel 11 does it appear that the King of the North has overwhelmed and vanquished all countries and opposition? Why, yes, of course, this is not fulfilled until we come to Daniel 11:45.

At this point, even without our exposition illustrating the "how, when, and where" of the verb "enter" (when Rome is to commence her spiritual, military onslaught in total transparency before the world), it is now clear that the latter part of verse 40 of Daniel 11 is none other than an overview. Daniel then symbolically sets forth in verses 41–45 and 12:1–3 the remaining events that are to transpire in their chronological order. It has been necessary to set this foundation so that the commencement of these events will be clear to all.

**Dan. 11:41 "He shall enter[935] also into the glorious[6643] land,[776] and many[7227] countries shall be overthrown:[3782] but these[428] shall escape[4422] out of his hand,[4480], [3027] even Edom,[123] and Moab,[4124] and the chief[7225] of the children[1121] of Ammon."[5983]**

**DAN. 11:41…"HE shall ENTER" …**

As in verse forty, "enter" means "to besiege" or "to surround." The time and place of that action will be explained to the reader's satisfaction immediately after it is established who and what the glorious land is that "He" (Rome) is to enter.

## DAN. 11:41…"ALSO" …

In Daniel 11:41–42, the word "also" (the Hebrew word *gam*) has been used by some for a foundation to build upon, but this word does not exist in the original Hebrew in either verse. The translators have supplied it.

## DAN. 11:41…"into THE GLORIOUS LAND" …

Daniel 11:41 tells us "He (Rome) shall enter into the glorious land." The glorious land has met with much unnecessary conjecture as to its Biblical identity, all stemming from neglecting to follow the guidelines of Biblical hermeneutics. The glorious land has many different terms or titles, as we are about to see, but only one identity. Such is the case of the Lord Jesus Christ, having many different titles, for He performs many different roles, but He is only one Lord. His identity never changes.

Only by following correct Biblical hermeneutics or guidelines can one hope to identify the symbols correctly and thus interpret the text aright. In demonstrating those Biblical principles again we restate how the things of God before the cross are always taken in a literal and local sense and, after the cross, in a symbolic or spiritual, worldwide sense. For example, in Daniel 10:14 and 11:14, we interpret "thy people" as meaning the literal Jews, and rightly so. But in Daniel 12:1, we interpret "thy people" as the saints of God, born-again Christians, spiritual Israel, the worldwide Christian Church at the very end of probationary time. In another instance, Paul explained that after the cross a Jew is not someone who is such merely by birth, but a Jew is the person who is circumcised or renewed in heart. This is the born-again Christian. He or she has become a spiritual Jew. The term "Jew" under this present dispensation now has a spiritual, worldwide application, but its identity never changes.

The same principle applies to the literal city, Jerusalem, which is now interpreted and understood to mean spiritual, worldwide Jerusalem, the Christian Church, but once again its identity never changes. And the principle with Babylon is the same, as well. After the cross, Babylon is no longer understood and confined to a literal, local, geographical location. No, Babylon, like the Jew and Jerusalem, is understood as spiritual, worldwide Babylon. In like manner, the same Biblical hermeneutical principle applies to the King of the South as well as to the King of the North and others. Before the cross: literal, local. After the cross: spiritual, worldwide. After the second coming: literal, local (the thousand-year millennium is literally 1000 years), but their identity never changes.

Louis F. Were illustrates this principal quite correctly:

> "There is no change in the phraseology employed in the New Testament, but there is positively a change regarding the people to whom those prophecies and designations now apply. In the New Testament, the church is spoken of in the language employed in the Old Testament concerning Israel."[13]

Another illustration that will serve us well is found in the Old Testament. Israel is referred to as "the people of the Lord," not the land of the Lord, because Israel is a term used for the church, as we will shortly demonstrate:

> "And Moses and the priests the Levites spake unto all Israel, saying, Take heed, and hearken, O Israel; this day thou art become the people of the LORD thy God." Deut 27:9.

We shall view some of the terms employed in the Old Testament representing the church of Israel, but first we must ask ourselves what Daniel understood the "glorious land" to be. Did he consider it the realm of the church, or perhaps the USA? What is the truth of this matter? Let us proceed then to disclose the true identity of the glorious land, for without its Biblical identity we cannot know what the King of the North is to "enter." Our first step is to see if Daniel has previously used the phrase. We find that he has—in the very same chapter:

> Daniel 11:16 "But he that cometh against him shall do according to His own will, and none shall stand before him: and he shall stand in the glorious land, which by his hands shall be consumed." (See margin KJV for terms used for the same entity: the land of ornament or goodly. Compare margin of Daniel 11:41—goodly land, land of delight, or, ornament—more on this later.)

---

13 *The Moral Purpose of Prophecy*, 30.

The precise terminology, "the glorious land," as found in the Bible, is found only in Daniel 11:16, 41. Although no closer yet to a definition, we nevertheless find Ezekiel using almost identical language for the same symbol, thus revealing a definitive clue for our identification:

> "In the day that I lifted up mine hand unto them, to bring them forth of the land of Egypt into a land that I had espied for them, flowing with milk and honey, which is the glory of all lands." Ezekiel 20:6.

What is the land of "milk and honey," which is the glory of all lands or, as we will see, the "glorious land"?

"The people rejoiced that they were to come into possession of so *goodly a land*, and they listened intently as the report was brought to Moses, that not a word should escape them. "We came unto the land whither thou sentest us," the spies began, "and surely it floweth with *milk and honey*; and this is the fruit of it." The people were enthusiastic; they would eagerly obey the voice of the Lord and go up at once to possess the land. But after describing the beauty and fertility of the land, all but two of the spies enlarged upon the difficulties and dangers that lay before the Israelites should they undertake the conquest of *Canaan*."[14]

Plainly, Canaan is the land of "milk and honey," the glory of all lands. However, Ellen White left with us a distinct clue supporting the link of "the glorious land" of Daniel 11:16, 41 to Canaan, the land of "milk and honey."

It is interesting to note that in the Old Testament the noun:

> "milk" [4612] is translated to designate "an office, a position, a place. It is used of the placement and service of a group of people....It is used of positions held by a group of people...or a single individual."[15]

---

14   Ellen White, *Patriarchs and Prophets*, 387–8.

15   Warren Baker and Eugene Carpenter, *The Complete Word Study Dictionary: OldTestament*, (Chattanooga: AMG Publishers, 2003), 644.

While she never used the specific term "the glorious land," she did use its equivalent "the goodly land," which we read in the marginal readings of Daniel 11:16, 41. What then does this connection imply? Let us allow Ellen White to explain this herself as we share with the reader two quotes that will give us our definitive definition beyond doubt:

> "And David looked around him upon the costly buildings of cedar, the homes of the inhabitants settled in the *goodly land* of *Canaan*, and conceived the idea that a temple should be built, more worthy for the residence of God. The site of the building was indicated and the most complete instructions were given, and Solomon entered upon the great work."[16]

> "I have tried to bring back a good report and a few grapes from the *heavenly Canaan*, for which many would stone me, as the congregation bade stone Caleb and Joshua for their report. (Num. 14:10.) But I declare to you, my brethren and sisters in the Lord, it is a *goodly land*, and we are well able to go up and possess it."[17]

From these two quotes we have the *"goodly land"* of *Canaan* directly connected to the temple here on the earth (Jerusalem) and the other one in heaven (Jerusalem). Paul eliminates any confusion by stating that the church on earth and the church in heaven are one and the same church:

> "But ye are come unto mount Sion, and unto the city of the living God, the heavenly Jerusalem, and to an enumerable company of angels, To the general assembly and church of the firstborn, which are written in heaven, and to God the Judge of all, and to the spirits of just men made perfect." Hebrews 12:22–23.

Ellen White is in total agreement with Paul. Notice the following statements:

---

16   Ellen White, *Manuscript Releases,* 3:230.
17   Ellen White, *Early Writings,* 14.

"Believers on the earth and those who have never fallen in heaven are one church."[18]

"The church is God's fortress. His city of refuge, which He holds in a revolted world. Any betrayal of the church is treachery to Him who has bought mankind with the blood of His only-begotten Son. From the beginning, faithful souls have constituted the church on earth. In every age the Lord has had His watchmen, who have borne a faithful testimony to the generation in which they lived. These sentinels gave the message of warning; and when they were called to lay off their armor, others took up the work. God brought these witnesses into covenant relation with Himself, *uniting the church on earth with the church in heaven.* He has sent forth His angels to minister to His church, and the gates of hell have not been able to prevail against His people."[19]

With a "thus saith the Lord" firmly established for those terms examined in Daniel 11:16 and 41, we have represented and established a clear definition for "the glorious land." It is the church of Christ.

Further support for this interpretation is forthcoming. However, we need now to look at another term used in conjunction with Christ's church. Please note that Paul refers to the church, the heavenly Jerusalem, as a city. What does a city denote in prophecy? A church:

"But the court which is without the temple leave out, and measure it not; for it is given unto the Gentiles: and the holy city shall they tread under foot forty [and] two months." Rev.11:2.

The seventh volume of the *Seventh-day Adventist Bible Commentary*, page 560, tells us more about spiritual Jerusalem:

"Sion. Or, 'Zion,' a poetic name for Jerusalem (see on Ps. 48:2; cf. Heb. 12:22)."

---

18   Ellen White, *Manuscript Releases,* 9:91.

19   Ellen White, *Acts of the Apostles,* 11.

"Beautiful for situation, the joy of the whole earth, is mount Zion, on the sides of the north, the city of the great King." Ps. 48:2.

In chapter 8, Daniel introduces another aspect for our understanding in his use of the phrase "the pleasant land:"

"And out of one of them came forth a little horn, which waxed exceeding great, toward the south, and toward the east, and toward the pleasant land." Dan. 8:9.

Jeremiah uses the same term:

"But I said, How shall I put thee among the children, and give thee a pleasant land, a goodly heritage of the hosts of nations? and I said, Thou shalt call me, My father; and shalt not turn away from me." Jer. 3:19.

The "pleasant land," a "goodly heritage," is none other than a term for Palestine. According to the *Seventh-day Adventist Bible Dictionary*, Volume 8, under the heading "Canaan," one reads the definition: "the biblical name of Palestine."

We must also keep in mind that the church of the Old Testament was a theocracy, and it extended to the borders of Palestine.

"The children of Israel were to occupy all the territory which God appointed them."[20]

"Thus the whole land, under God's control, would become an object lesson of spiritual truth."[21]

The term Palestine was exclusively used in connection with the Jews:

"There are those who hold that the Sabbath was given only for the Jews; but God has never said this. He committed the Sabbath to his people Israel as a sacred trust; but the very fact that the desert of Sinai, and not *Palestine*, was the place selected by him in which to proclaim his law, reveals that he intended it for all mankind. The law of ten commandments is as old as

---

20   Ellen White, *Christ's Object Lessons,* 290.

21   Ellen White, *Christ's Object Lessons,* 289.

creation. Therefore the Sabbath institution has no special relation to the Jews, any more than to all other created beings."[22]

"It may be surprising to some that Christ's work was confined to so small a circumference, that it was not extended to the
heathen nations surrounding Palestine. But the heathen nations
were not prepared for his work. And had he devoted his time
to the conversion of the Gentile world, he would have closed
the door whereby he could bear his message to the Jewish nation."[23]

We find further confirmation with these quotations:

"Paul's great object in visiting Jerusalem was to conciliate
the church of Palestine."[24]

"The disciples were to begin their work by publishing the
great truths of Christianity in the metropolis of Palestine, and
from Jerusalem they were to go to all parts of the world."[25]

"In the past the labors of the apostles had been put forth
wholly in Palestine. Round this place their hopes had clustered.
They regarded the Jews as the covenant people of God."[26]

"The Jews were regarded as the covenant people of God
because "to this people were committed the oracles of God."[27]

This segment of our study brings to light the fact that in no
uncertain terms is any person authorized to give a new meaning
to a term whose definition is already clearly established in the
Bible and the Spirit of Prophecy. To say that the glorious land
and/or goodly land is the United States of America is to ignore
the hermeneutical principle laid down for us by the scriptures and
Inspiration. To step off this platform, we believe, would open the
floodgates of speculation and, in fact, it has, causing many to be

---

22  Ellen White, *Review and Herald,* August 30, 1898.

23  Ellen White, *Signs of the Times,* December 16, 1897.

24  Ellen White, *Sketches from the Life of Paul,* 214.

25  Ellen White, *Manuscript Releases,* 12:307.

26  Ellen White, *Youth Instructor,* November 15, 1900.

27  Ellen White, *Christ's Object Lessons,* 287.

misled. We cannot say the glorious land and/or the goodly land in Daniel 11:16 represents the Jews, God's people, His church; and then say the same symbol in Daniel 11:41 now represents the United States of America, a civil entity. We are not at liberty to change the identity of a heaven-defined symbol, we may only define its literal or spiritual application. Changing the identity would be confusion compounded. Let us stay within the parameters of that which is defined in the scriptures, for therein lies our only safety and due course. Now that the "glorious land" is described as a term designated for the church (and we will have more to say on this topic), why does the Bible use the term "glorious" to define His last day church in the book of Daniel? Turning to a chapter in *Christ Object Lessons* entitled *"The Lord's Vineyard,"* His church; Ellen White clarifies the matter for us:

"The parable of the vineyard applies not alone to the Jewish nation. It has a lesson for us. *The church* in this generation has been endowed by God with great privileges and blessings, and He expects corresponding returns....The husbandman chooses a *piece of land* from the wilderness; he fences, clears, and tills it, and plants it with choice vines, expecting a rich harvest. This plot of ground, in its superiority to the uncultivated waste, he expects to do him honor by showing the results of his care and toil in its cultivation. So God had chosen a people from the world to be trained and educated by Christ. The prophet says, 'The vineyard of the Lord of hosts is the house of Israel, and the men of Judah His pleasant plant.' Isa. 5:7. [This piece of land is the same as in Daniel 8:9, the "pleasant land"] Upon this people God had bestowed great privileges, blessing them richly from His abundant goodness. He looked for them to honor Him by yielding fruit. *They were to reveal the principles of His kingdom.* In the midst of a fallen, wicked world *they were to represent the character of God.* As the Lord's vineyard they were to produce fruit altogether different from that of the heathen nations....

"It was the privilege of the Jewish nation to *represent the character of God as it had been revealed to Moses.* In answer to the prayer of Moses, 'Show me *Thy glory*,' the Lord promised, 'I will make all My goodness pass before thee. Ex. 33:18, 19. 'And the Lord passed by before him, and proclaimed, The Lord, the Lord God, merciful and gracious, longsuffering, and abundant in goodness and truth, keeping mercy for thousands, forgiving iniquity and transgression and sin.' Ex. 34:6, 7. *This was the fruit that God desired from His people.* In the *purity of their characters*, in the *holiness of their lives*, in their *mercy* and *loving-kindness* and *compassion*, they were to show that 'the law of the Lord is perfect, converting the soul.' Ps. 19:7.

"Through the Jewish nation it was God's purpose to impart rich blessings to all peoples. *Through Israel the way was to be prepared for the diffusion of His light to the whole world.* The nations of the world, through following corrupt practices, had lost the knowledge of God. Yet in His mercy God did not blot them out of existence. *He purposed to give them opportunity for becoming acquainted with Him through His church.* He designed that the principles revealed through His people should be the means of restoring the moral image of God in man..... And as the tower in the vineyard, *God placed in the midst of the land His holy temple.....* God desired to make of *His people Israel a praise and a glory.* Every spiritual advantage was given them. *God withheld from them nothing favorable to the formation of character that would make them representatives of Himself.* Their obedience to the law of God would make them marvels of prosperity before the nations of the world...*The glory of God,* His majesty and power, were to be revealed in all their prosperity. *They were to be a kingdom of priests and princes.* God furnished them with every facility for becoming the greatest nation on the earth..... *the people were to reflect the attributes of His character.*

"Even the heathen would recognize the superiority of those who served and worshiped the living God....*The children of Israel were to occupy all the territory which God appointed them* [His church]. Those nations that rejected the worship and service of the true God were to be dispossessed. *But it was God's purpose that by the revelation of His character through Israel men should be drawn unto Him....He desires that the families below shall be a symbol of the great family above. ...*But Israel did not fulfill God's purpose....All their advantages were appropriated for their *own glorification....They robbed God of the service He required of them, and they robbed their fellow men of religious guidance and a holy example....*Like the inhabitants of the antediluvian world, they followed out every imagination of their evil hearts. Thus they made sacred things appear a farce, saying, "The temple of the Lord, the temple of the Lord, are these" (Jer. 7:4), while at the same time *they were misrepresenting God's character,* dishonoring His name, and polluting His sanctuary..... *Thus the Gentile world was given occasion to misinterpret the character of God and the laws of His kingdom*...

"*The Jewish rulers did not love God....The Jewish people cherished the idea that they were the favorites of heaven, and that they were always to be exalted as the church of God....*As a people the Jews had failed of fulfilling God's purpose, and the vineyard was taken from them. The privileges they had abused, the work they had slighted, was entrusted to others...."

Ellen White now describes the church of today:

"In the lives of God's people the truths of His word are to reveal their *glory* and *excellence. Through His people Christ is to manifest His character and the principles of His kingdom.... The Lord desires through His people to answer Satan's charges by showing the results of obedience to right principles.* These principles are to be manifest in the individual Christian, in the family, in the church, and in every institution established for God's service....*Not all the beauty of art can bear comparison with the beauty of temper and character to be revealed in those who are Christ's representatives....*We are to praise God by tangible service, *by doing all in our power to advance the glory of His name.* God imparts His gifts to us that we also may give, and thus make known *His character to the world....*God claims the whole earth as His vineyard. Though now in the hands of the usurper, it belongs to God....

"Yet the world is asleep. The people know not the time of their visitation. *In this crisis, where is the church to be found? Are its members meeting the claims of God? Are they fulfilling His commission, and representing His character to the world?... The glorious possibilities set before Israel could be realized only through obedience to God's commandments. The same elevation of character, the same fulness of blessing—blessing on mind and soul and body, blessing on house and field, blessing for this life and for the life to come—is possible for us only through obedience. In the spiritual as in the natural world, obedience to the laws of God is the condition of fruit bearing. And when men teach the people to disregard God's commandments, they are preventing them from bearing fruit to His glory.*"[28]

---

28  Ellen White, *Christ's Object Lessons,* 284–306. (All emphasis mine).

Paul admonishes us to glorify God in everything we do including our spiritual, mental and physical well being and to be blameless at His appearing:

> "And the very God of peace sanctify you wholly; and I pray God your whole spirit and soul and body be preserved blameless unto the coming of our Lord Jesus Christ." 1Thess. 5:23.

> "In Egypt their taste had become perverted. God designed to restore their appetite to a pure, healthy state, in order that they might enjoy the simple fruits that were given to Adam and Eve in Eden. He was about to establish them in a *second Eden*, a *goodly land*, where they might enjoy the fruits and grains that He would provide for them. He purposed to remove the feverish diet upon which they had subsisted in Egypt; for He wished them to be in perfect health and soundness when they entered the *goodly land* to which He was leading them, so that the surrounding heathen nations might be constrained to *glorify the God of Israel*, the God who had done so wonderful a work for His people. Unless the people who acknowledged Him as the God of heaven were in *perfect soundness of health, His name could not be glorified.*"[29]

In Ps. 96:3 we are commissioned to "Declare His glory [character] among the nations." And John also in the very end of time declares we are to "give him glory" [by reflecting His character] Rev. 14:7. Daniel presents the character for those who would be endowed with the Holy Spirit when the church is to meet her enemies in the final onslaught with the forces of evil just before she is to enter the promised land. The condition is summarized here:

> "The great work of life is character building…"[30]

Here, then, lies the most important aspect of Daniel 11 and why Satan would introduce a counterfeit of so great a magnitude. In Daniel 1 we have the history of the Jews being taken captive, but we were not specifically told why in that chapter. That reason is addressed here:

---

29    *Seventh-Day Adventist Bible Commentary*, 1:1102.

30    Ellen White, *Patriarchs and Prophets*, 596.

"By their spirit and works the children of Israel *misrepresented the righteousness of God's character*, and the Lord allowed the Babylonians to take them captive. He left his people to their ways; and in the calamities that befell them the innocent suffered with the guilty."[31]

It was all because of a misrepresentation of God's character to the surrounding nations. And to us the message is made plain:

"Now all these things happened unto them for ensamples: and they are written for our admonition, upon whom the ends of the world are come." 1 Cor. 10:11.

And we all know that:

"The conditions and promises are the same in the Old Testament as they are in the New. The favor of God is promised only to those who obey him."[32]

Let us take heed then for we have an admonition that no one can misunderstand. John complements Daniel in Revelation 14:1:

"And I looked, and, lo, a Lamb stood on the mount Sion, and with him an hundred forty and four thousand, having his *Father's name written in their foreheads*."

A name denotes character, and having the Father's name written in one's forehead denotes having His glorious character exemplified in one's life. In Revelation 14 we have the clearest instruction for those who will act a part in the proclamation of the last warning messages to the world, and the condition for those who will be able to stand when Michael Himself will stand up, Daniel 12:1. Many are now hidden, but nevertheless His glorious church will arise and their light will shine forth:

"Arise, shine; for thy light is come, and the glory of the LORD is risen upon thee." "For, behold, the darkness shall cover the earth, and gross darkness the people: but the LORD

---

31   Ellen White, *Youth Instructor,* May 14, 1903.

32   Ellen White, *Signs of the Times,* January 6, 1888.

shall arise upon thee, and his glory shall be seen upon thee."
Isa. 60:1–2.

Ellen White describes this glorious ascent of the church in the following excerpts:

> "Christ's true followers are *kind, tender, pitiful.* They will realize the meaning of the work of the angel of Revelation 18, who is to *lighten the whole earth with his glory*, while he cries with a loud voice, 'Babylon the great is fallen, is fallen.' Many will heed this call....When the earth is *lighted with the glory of the angel of Revelation 18*, the religious elements, good and evil, will awake from slumber, and the armies of the living God will take the field."[33]

> "During the loud cry, the church, aided by the providential interpositions of her exalted Lord, will diffuse the knowledge of salvation so abundantly that light will be communicated to every city and town. The earth will be filled with the knowledge of salvation. So abundantly will the renewing Spirit of God have crowned with success the intensely active agencies, that the light of present truth will be seen flashing everywhere."[34]

> "The message of Christ's righteousness is to sound from one end of the earth to the other to prepare the way of the Lord. This is the glory of God, which closes the work of the third angel."[35]

> *"When the Lord was about to manifest to them his great power and goodness, to make his name glorious in the earth, and exalt his people as a nation favored and honored of Heaven*, they became discouraged. They knew that whenever they had trusted in God he had mightily wrought for them. Yet their unbelief strengthened into rebellion; their own perverse wills obstructed the way, making walls before them higher than had been built by their enemies.
> "The history of the children of Israel is written as a warning to us, 'upon whom the ends of the world are come.' We are standing, as it were, upon the very borders of the *heavenly*

---

33   Ellen White, *Manuscript Releases,* 19:159–60.

34   Ellen White, *Review and Herald*, Oct. 13, 1904.

35   Ellen White, *Testimonies for the Church,* 6:19.

*Canaan.* We may, if we will, look over on the other side, and behold the attractions of the *goodly land.* If we have faith in the promises of God, we shall show in conversation and in deportment that we are not living for this world, but are making it our first business to prepare for that *holy land.*

"The dangers and difficulties before us are increasing as we near the *heavenly rest.* Satan is filled with deadly hatred against all who are seeking to gain *the land* which was *once his home.* His envy has lost none of its bitterness since he was excluded from the brightness and *glory* of Heaven. Before his fall an enemy to Christ, seeking to rob him of his honor and *glory*, he is no less his enemy now. He has determined to take the world captive. He sees that his time is short, that a mightier than he will soon take away his power, and he will make one last mighty effort against *Christ and his church.*"[36]

"The third angel's message is to lighten the earth with its *glory*; but only those who have withstood temptation in the strength of the Mighty One will be permitted to act a part in proclaiming it when it shall have swelled into the loud cry."[37]

Our instruction for preparation is clearly set before us. The Jews, we were told, did not love God; therefore, it was impossible for them to reflect His glory or character to the surrounding nations. Hence they failed to comprehend and experience that obedience to God's commands springs forth only after one experiences supreme love for God. According to the scriptures, this is the very *root* and foundation for the born-again Christian:

Matt. 13:21 "Yet hath he not root in himself, but dureth for a while: for when tribulation or persecution ariseth because of the word, by and by he is offended."

Eph. 3:17 "That Christ may dwell in your hearts by faith; that ye, being rooted and grounded in love...."

After being beaten, stoned, imprisoned, and shipwrecked and the like, what was Paul's secret for not harboring a bitter spirit and forsaking his Lord?

---

36  Ellen White, *Review and Herald,* November 29, 1881.

37  Ellen White, *Historical Sketches,* 155.

"For the love of Christ constraineth us." 2 Cor. 5:14.

His answer was simple, yet profound. It should be no wonder, then, why Paul would exclaim in summation:

> "Though I speak with the tongues of men and of angels, and have not charity, I am become as sounding brass, or a tinkling cymbal. And though I have the gift of prophecy, and understand all mysteries, and all knowledge; and though I have all faith, so that I could remove mountains, and have not charity, I am nothing. And though I bestow all my goods to feed the poor, and though I give my body to be burned, and have not charity, it profiteth me nothing." 1 Cor. 13:1–3.

It was this strong motivating principal of supreme love for God that prepared Shadrach, Meshach, and Abednego not to bow to the king's image, and enabled them to accept without hesitation the fiery trial resulting from their refusal. On a daily basis they had faithfully lived the principles of righteousness in truth, thus sealing their fate in that hour of temptation.

> "Lo, I see four men loose, walking in the midst of the fire, and they have no hurt; and the form of the fourth is like the Son of God.' How did that heathen king know what the Son of God was like? The Hebrew captives filling positions of trust in Babylon had in life and character represented before him the truth. When asked for a reason of their faith, they had given it without hesitation. Plainly and simply they had presented the principles of righteousness, thus teaching those around them of the God whom they worshiped. They had told of Christ, the Redeemer to come; and in the form of the fourth in the midst of the fire the king recognized the Son of God."[38]

The last term mentioned in the margins of Daniel 11:16 and 41 was the "land of ornament." What was the ornament that God wanted to extend to the borders of Palestine and beyond?

> Prov. 4:9. "She [Wisdom] shall give to thine head an ornament of grace: a crown of glory shall she deliver to thee."

---

38   Ellen White, *Prophets and Kings*, 509.

> Isa. 61:10. "I will greatly rejoice in the LORD, my soul shall be joyful in my God; for he hath clothed me with the garments of salvation, he hath covered me with the robe of righteousness, as a bridegroom decketh himself with ornaments, and as a bride adorneth herself with her jewels."

And what did John say is the covering or "ornament" of salvation for the born-again Christian?

> Rev. 19:8. "And to her was granted that she should be arrayed in fine linen, clean and white: for the fine linen is the righteousness of saints."

The ornament of salvation or glory that is to shine and sound from one end of the earth to the other in the soon-coming crisis is none other than Christ and His righteousness, exhibited through the persons and characters of His witnesses, His church. Therefore, Paul:

> "Encouraged the believers to look forward to the time when Christ, who 'loved the church, and gave Himself for it,' would 'present it to Himself a *glorious church* [and/or the glorious land], not having spot, or wrinkle, or any such thing'—a church 'holy and without blemish.' Ephesians 5:25, 27."[39]

Having allowed the scriptures and Spirit of Prophecy to interpret themselves it is transparently clear that when Rome invades the "glorious land," she is invading the realm of the church.

Before moving away from this topic we must first address an issue that requires further clarification when the King of the North is to "enter into the glorious land."

According to Dan.11:40, when, the King of the North (the papacy) was to "overflow and pass over." This is a description of total victory, as we have already illustrated. Nothing can stand in Rome's way; complete annihilation, unqualified subjection, national submission, is hereby described, for it affords no other interpretation.

How, then, does one integrate the following facts to support the supposition of those who interpret Dan. 11:40 in chronological

---

39   Ellen White, *Acts of the Apostles*, 470.

order? That view is that the King of the South (atheistic communism, represented by Russia) came to his end at the hands of the King of the North in 1989. But imagine if you can, a military conquest without loss of life or a single shot being fired, and compare that view with the merciless, relentless actions of the King of the North depicted in the prophecy. Also, according to that interpretation, Russia must remain a conquered, impotent nation, no more to be a player but a pawn in history, all the way up to Daniel 12:1, when Michael will stand up at the close of probation, and to the second coming, as well. Let us see if that interpretation will stand the test of investigation.

First, do the following news articles confirm Russia as a defeated, subordinate nation? Do they describe the results of complete and permanent submission of atheistic communism in 1989 to the overwhelming force described in Dan 11:40?:

### *"Russia Deploys New Set Of Nuclear Missiles; More to Come*

"'This is the most advanced state-of-the-art missile in the world,' Ivanov said. 'Only such weapons can ensure and guarantee our sovereignty and security and make any attempts to put military pressure on Russia absolutely senseless.'...The Topol-M missiles, capable of hitting targets more than 6,000 miles away, have so far been deployed in silos. The mobile version is set to become operational next year, said the Strategic Missile Forces chief, Col. Gen. Nikolai Solovtsov....Next year, design work will start on a next-generation heavy nuclear missile, which will enter service after 2009, the General Staff officer said. The new missile will be capable of carrying 10 nuclear warheads with a total weight of up to 4.4 tons. The Topol-M's combat payload is 1.32 tons, he added." [40]

### *"Russia Tests "Father of All Bombs"*

"Russia has tested the world's most powerful vacuum bomb, which unleashes a destructive shockwave with the power of a nuclear blast but which it says is much more environmentally friendly. The bomb is the latest in a series of new Russian weap-

---

40   *The Columbus Dispatch,* December 23, 2003.

ons and policy moves as President Vladimir Putin tries to reassert Moscow's role on the international stage. The military has dubbed it the 'father of all bombs' because it is much stronger than the US-built Massive Ordnance Air Blast bomb—MOAB, also known under its name 'Mother of All Bombs.'

"'Test results of the new airborne weapon have shown that its efficiency and power is commensurate with a nuclear weapon,' Alexander Rukshin, Russian deputy armed forces chief of staff, told Russia's state ORT First Channel television.... 'The defence ministry stresses this military invention does not contradict a single international treaty. Russia is not unleashing a new arms race.'

"'The main destruction is inflicted by an ultrasonic shockwave and an incredibly high temperature,' the reports said. 'All that is alive merely evaporates.' Mr Rukshin said: 'At the same time, I want to stress that the action of this weapon does not contaminate the environment, in contrast to a nuclear one.'

"The Tu-160 supersonic bomber that dropped the [test] bomb, widely known under its NATO nickname of 'Blackjack,' is the heaviest combat aircraft ever built. Putin, who has overseen the roll-out of new tactical and anti-aircraft missiles and combat aircraft, has ordered 'Blackjacks' and the Tu-95 'Bear' bombers to patrol around the world."[41]

And we shall not forget to mention Russia's Typhoon-class submarines, the world's largest, and one of the most powerful military machines ever.

### *"Fears of New Cold War as Russia Threatens to Switch Off the Gas*

"At 10am on Sunday, Russia is threatening to unleash the most powerful weapon in its post-Soviet arsenal: unless Ukraine agrees to a fourfold increase in the price it pays for gas, Russia will simply turn off the tap.

"Nor is it just Ukraine under threat—the EU imports about half of its gas from Russia and 80 per cent of that comes through Ukrainian pipelines.

"So when President Putin met Ivan Plachkov, the Ukrainian Energy Minister, in Moscow yesterday, there was more at stake than relations between the neighbouring states. Analysts

41   *The Daily Telegraph*, September 12, 2007.

fear the dispute could provide a foretaste of how Russia will use its massive oil and gas reserves as a foreign policy tool in future disputes with the West. The Russian authorities are also threatening BP over alleged environmental violations on a Siberian field in what is seen as a wider attempt to seize back assets handed over to foreign companies when energy prices were low."[42]

## *"$20bn Gas Project Seized by Russia*

"Shell is being forced by the Russian government to hand over its controlling stake in the world's biggest liquefied gas project, provoking fresh fears about the Kremlin's willingness to use the country's growing strength in natural resources as a political weapon. After months of relentless pressure from Moscow, the Anglo-Dutch company has to cut its stake in the $20bn Sakhalin-2 scheme in the far east of Russia in favour of the state-owned energy group Gazprom...."[43]

## *"Russia Signs Deal to Bring Natural Gas Pipeline through Bulgaria*

"Russia strengthened its grip over Europe's energy supplies Friday as it signed a major natural gas deal with Bulgaria in a move that analysts said would further undermine the European Union's attempts to diversify its energy sources....'Russia has an almost full monopoly over Bulgaria's energy market and the EU shockingly acts like a naïve bystander, completely blind to the major strategic reconfiguration that is taking place in the Balkans,' Minchev said....Russia is poised to take over the state-owned Petroleum Industry of Serbia, known as NIS...."[44]

In view of this evidence, what kind of credibility would we have if we were to claim that Russia is a defeated nation? Have the specifications of the prophecy aligned themselves with the facts under investigation?

---

42  *The Times*, December 30, 2005.

43  *The Guardian*, December 12, 2006.

44  *The International Herald Tribune*, January 18, 2008.

While we fully acknowledge that Russia experienced a serious downturn in 1989, in no wise can it be shown that she experienced complete annihilation, whether militarily, economically, politically or even religiously, in that she had no further resources or will for resistance or aggression, as the prophecy demands. In fact, no other country today is building up its military strength with such speed as Russia. And as a result of petrodollars from Europe and abroad flowing into this oil- and gas-rich nation's coffers, she has the economic power to flex her political muscles, as well.

The Bible and the Spirit of Prophecy are most definitive that the warfare pursued by the King of the North is indeed spiritual (with state and perhaps even military backing), but it will be *religious* in nature—a religious coup, so to speak. We therefore inquire, "Is there a Sunday law in Russia today?" Has Russia bowed to the papal will in this ultimate regard? And if the papacy, the King of the North, somehow "overthrew and passed over" Russia in 1989, why is it that the pope himself has not been able, for the last 25 years, to even enter the country?:

### *"Gesture Doesn't Get Pope Visit to Russia*

"VATICAN CITY (AP) — Pope John Paul II met with Russian President Vladimir Putin yesterday and made a gesture in hopes of improving relations with the Russian Orthodox Church, but Putin did not invite him to Russia in return.

"John Paul has made improving relations with the Orthodox Church a priority of his 25-year papacy, but his long-sought dream of visiting Russia has been blocked by the Russian Orthodox Church, which is wary of advances by Roman Catholics since the fall of communism....Putin told Italian reporters in Moscow he wanted to help end the dispute between the Vatican and the Orthodox Church. "'I see my task not in ensuring the pope's visit to Russia, but in helping these steps toward unity,' he said.'"[45]

All are agreed that the Sunday law finds its commencement first in the USA. According to *Testimonies for the Church,* 6:18, 395: "Every country on the globe will be led to follow her [America's] example." "*Every country on the globe*"—and this

---

45    *The Columbus Dispatch,* November 6, 2003.

includes *all* countries representing atheistic communism as well. The "overflowing and passing over" of a subordinated, religious-ly-conquered Russia does not come until then. Neither the Bible nor the Spirit of Prophecy declares that Rome will strike before the deadly wound is to be healed. And when Rome does strike, are we to believe Russia will be the first to be confronted by the King of the North? No. Atheistic communism, as well as all the other nations (presently there are over 200 in all), does not even come into the prophetic picture until we first see a national Sunday law in America. This we will show from the Bible, as well. It is time to find a suitable interpretation.

Inspiration has informed us that the time is coming when Rome is to strike. This has been illustrated elsewhere; however, let us view the matter in its entirety so we can know when, where, and how Rome "enters" to overthrow God's church:

> "Church and state are now making preparations for the future conflict. Protestants are working in disguise to bring Sunday to the front, as did the Romanists. Throughout the land the papacy is piling up her lofty and massive structures, in the secret recesses of which her former persecutions are to be re-peated."[46]

> "Protestants little know what they are doing when they propose to accept the aid of Rome in the work of Sunday ex-altation. While they are bent upon the accomplishment of their purpose, Rome is aiming to re-establish her power, to recover her lost supremacy. Let the principle once be established in the United States that the church may employ or control the power of the state; that religious observances may be enforced by secular laws; in short, that the authority of church and state is to dominate the conscience, and the triumph of Rome in this country is assured.

> "God's word has given warning of the impending dan-ger; let this be unheeded, and the Protestant world will learn what the purposes of Rome really are, only when it is too late to escape the snare. She is silently growing into power. Her doctrines are exerting their influence in legislative halls, in the churches, and in the hearts of men. She is piling up her lofty and massive structures in the secret recesses of which her former

---

46   Ellen White, *Testimonies for the Church*, 5:449–50.

persecutions will be repeated. Stealthily and unsuspectedly she is strengthening her forces to further her own ends when the time shall come for her to *strike*."[47]

Did you notice that before the strike can take place, "the authority of church and state is to dominate the conscience"? That means a union of church and state is first to take place, and then "the triumph of Rome in this country is assured." Yet the strike is still placed in the future:

> "...Sunday observance owes its existence as a so-called Christian institution to 'the mystery of iniquity;' and its enforcement will be a virtual recognition of the principles which are the very cornerstone of Romanism. When our nation shall so abjure the principles of its government as to enact a Sunday law, Protestantism will in this act join hands with popery; it will be nothing else than giving life to the tyranny, which has long been eagerly watching its opportunity to spring again into active despotism.
> "...If popery or its principles shall again be legislated into power, the fires of persecution will be rekindled against those who will not sacrifice conscience and the truth in deference to popular errors. This evil is on the point of realization."[48]

We read of this very event in the Revelator's book:

> "And he had power to give life unto the image of the beast, that the image of the beast should speak, and cause that, as many as would not worship the image of the beast should be killed. And he causeth all, both small and great, rich and poor, free and bond, to receive a mark in their right hand, or in their foreheads." Rev. 13:15–16.

John says, "And he had power to give *life* unto the image...." Ellen White clarified it in this way: The Sunday law will be "nothing else than giving *life* to the tyranny which has long been eagerly watching its opportunity to spring again into active despotism." *How* will this take place? She leaves no doubt. *Through legislation*, when it shall be "legislated into power." The life that returns from the healing of the deadly wound is *when* a *national Sunday*

---

47  Ellen White, *Great Controversy*, 581.

48  Ellen White, *Testimonies for the Church*, 5:712.

*law*, essentially an ecclesiastical law, is legislated into civil law by the state, whereby resurrecting religious persecution. *Where* does one look for this resurrection, this union of church and state to first take place? *America*. Once this has been accomplished and the law is on the side of Rome, it will be seen that, at that time, Rome will strike. Thus commences the prophecy and the final onslaught against God's church by Rome, as delineated in Daniel 11:40–41. From this act Ellen White illustrates a parallel:

> "As the approach of the Roman armies was a sign to the disciples of the impending destruction of Jerusalem, so may this apostasy [the coming Sunday law] be a sign to us that the limit of God's forbearance is reached, that the measure of our nation's iniquity is full, and that the angel of mercy is about to take her flight, never to return."[49]

> "As the siege of Jerusalem by the Roman armies was the signal for flight to the Judean Christians, so the assumption of power on the part of our nation in the decree enforcing the papal sabbath will be a warning to us. It will then be time to leave the large cities, preparatory to leaving the smaller ones for retired homes in secluded places among the mountains."[50]

To understand our explicate counsel as a church in proclaiming the second and third angles messages when the crisis confronts God's people. **(See Appendix I, pg. 89)**.

We shall now address one last essential thought on the "glorious land" before we move on to our next clause in Daniel 11:41.

The two symbols designated by heaven for the church in Daniel 11 are "the glorious land," verses 16 and 41, and "the glorious holy mountain," verse 45. The two terms have several commonalities. Both are glorious; both are real estate; both verse 41 and 45 are symbolic. It is obvious two very similar entities are being described, and rightly so. They share a mutual identity—God's church—depicted by Daniel in two stages of its development. The first stage is the church militant; the second, the church trium-

---

49   Ellen White, *Testimonies for the Church*, 5:451

50   Ellen White, *Testimonies for the Church*, 5:464.

phant. The distinction between them is as important as their similarities. We are told:

"The Church militant is not the Church triumphant."[51]

They have their application in different time periods, as we will now show:

Dan. 11:45 "And he shall plant the tabernacles of his palace between the seas in the glorious holy mountain; yet he shall come to his end, and none shall help him."

What does a mountain represent in prophecy? A kingdom:

"Behold, I am against thee, O destroying mountain [Babylon], saith the LORD, which destroyest all the earth: and I will stretch out mine hand upon thee, and roll thee down from the rocks, and will make thee a burnt mountain." Jeremiah 51:25.

Why does Daniel call the church the "glorious holy mountain" in verse 45? Because the church is now the "church triumphant," although little beknownst to the people of God on earth at that time. Since a mountain in prophecy denotes a kingdom, Daniel's use of "glorious holy mountain" in verse 45 indicates God's kingdom has been made up. When does this occur? The answer should interest us mightily, as it pertains to our time. The latter portion of the verse tells us when it happens. Let's read it again:

Daniel 11:45 reads: "And he shall plant the tabernacles of his palace between the seas in the glorious holy mountain; yet he shall come to his end, and none shall help him."

God's kingdom is made up shortly before the power of the King of the North is broken. But when is *that* to take place? Let us read the answer in the very next verse:

"And at that time shall Michael stand up, the great prince which standeth for the children of thy people: and there shall be a time of trouble, such as never was since there was a nation even to that same time: and at that time thy people shall be

---

51   Ellen White, *Review and Herald,* December 31, 1901.

delivered, every one that shall be found written in the book."
Dan. 12:1.

The King of the North is broken at "that time" when Michael
stands up. That action closes human probation and starts the falling of the seven last plagues. The question that still remains to be
fully answered, though, is, "When is Christ's kingdom made up?"
Ellen White clarifies that it is when He pronounces:

> "He that is unjust, let him be unjust still: and he which is
> filthy, let him be filthy still: and he that is righteous, let him be
> righteous still: and he that is holy, let him be holy still."
>
> "Every case had been decided for life or death. While Jesus
> had been ministering in the sanctuary, the judgment had been
> going on for the righteous dead, and then for the righteous liv-
> ing. Christ had received His kingdom, having made the atone-
> ment for His people and blotted out their sins. The subjects of
> the kingdom were made up. The marriage of the Lamb was con-
> summated. And the kingdom, and the greatness of the kingdom
> under the whole heaven, was given to Jesus and the heirs of
> salvation, and Jesus was to reign as King of kings and Lord of
> lords."[52]

Isaiah 4:2–3 portrays God's church at that time as well:

> "In that day shall the branch of the LORD be beautiful and
> glorious....And it shall come to pass, that he that is left in Zion,
> and he that remaineth in Jerusalem, shall be called holy, even
> every one that is written among the living in Jerusalem."

The subjects of Christ's kingdom were all numbered, all those
since the days of Adam for whose sins He had atoned, including
all those still living that were sealed at "that time." The righteous
living and dead compose His kingdom, the "church triumphant,"
in place when Michael stood up—hence the appropriate symbol of
identity, "the glorious holy mountain." It will happen at the close
of probation. The reality of this will not be known or experienced
by humanity until the Second Coming of Christ.

On the other hand, "the church militant," termed in Daniel
11:41 "the glorious land," has its reference to an all-encompass-
ing, Christ-professing church. However, not all who profess to

---

52  Ellen White, *Early Writings*, 279–80.

be members of His church here on earth are counted as having citizenship in His heavenly church:

> "God has a church upon the earth who are His chosen people, who keep His commandments. He is leading, not stray offshoots, not one here and one there, but a people. The truth is a sanctifying power; but the church militant is not the church triumphant. There are tares among the wheat."[53]

> "Let everyone who is seeking to live a Christian life, re-member that the church militant is not the church triumphant. Those who are carnally minded will be found in the church. They are to be pitied more than blamed. The church is not to be judged as sustaining these characters, though they be found within her borders."[54]

This is clearly but sadly illustrated from those who lose their way all along the path:

> "The Bible will be opened from house to house, and men and women will find access to these homes, and minds will be opened to receive the word of God; and when the crisis comes, many will be prepared to make right decisions even in the face of the formidable difficulties that will be brought about through the deceptive miracles of Satan. Although these will confess the truth and become workers with Christ at the eleventh hour, they will receive equal wages with those who have wrought through the whole day. There will be an army of steadfast believers who will stand as firm as a rock through the last test. But where in that army are those who have been standard-bearers? Where are those whose voices have sounded in proclaiming the truth to the sinning? *Some of them are not there. We look for them, but in the time of shaking they have been unable to stand, and have passed over to the enemy's ranks.*"[55]

In verse 41, when the King of the North "enters"[935] (besieges, assaults, or surrounds) he is first seen assaulting the "glorious land," the church militant, Christ's commandment-keeping church. This crisis takes place first in America and then is witnessed throughout

---

53   Ellen White, *Testimonies to Ministers,* 61.

54   Ellen White, *Review and Herald,* January 16, 1894.

55   Ellen White, *Review and Herald,* December 24, 1889.

the rest of the world. We have already documented how the "same crisis will come upon our people in all parts of the world" because His church, spiritual Jerusalem, is scattered worldwide.

Here is where those who say the "glorious land" is the USA run into an irresolvable problem. Those who hold that position correctly interpret the prophecy in the particular that the assault explicitly comes *from* Rome *against* the "glorious land." However, after allowing Inspiration to describe the initial nature of America and her change in character, we will reveal the fundamental error of application made by those same individuals:

> "'And he had *two horns* like a lamb.' The lamblike horns indicate youth, innocence, and gentleness, fitly representing the character of the United States when presented to the prophet as 'coming up' in 1798. Among the Christian exiles who first fled to America and sought an asylum from royal oppression and priestly intolerance were many who determined to establish a government upon the broad foundation of civil and religious liberty. Their views found place in the Declaration of Independence, which sets forth the great truth that 'all men are created equal' and endowed with the inalienable right to 'life, liberty, and the pursuit of happiness.' And the Constitution guarantees to the people the right of self-government, providing that representatives elected by the popular vote shall enact and administer the laws. Freedom of religious faith was also granted, every man being permitted to worship God according to the dictates of his conscience. *Republicanism* and *Protestantism* became the *fundamental principles of the nation. These principles are the secret of its power and prosperity.*"[56]

Republicanism is the state or civil aspect of the USA. Protestantism is, of course, her religious aspect. The question, then, is very simple: Where is the evidence that it is the United States that is to be assaulted? In fact, we read a very different scenario:

> "Then the *Catholics bid the Protestants to go forward*, and issue a decree that all who will not observe the first day of the week, instead of the seventh day, shall be slain. And the Catholics, whose numbers are large, *will stand by the Protestants. The Catholics will give their power to the image of the beast.* And

---

56   Ellen White, *Great Controversy*, 441.

the Protestants will work as their mother worked before them to destroy the saints."[57]

When the Catholics "stand by the Protestants" and "give their power to the image of the beast," that obviously does not describe a military assault against apostate Protestantism. In fact, it is apostate Protestantism that will be first and foremost to "stretch her hand across the gulf to grasp the hand of the Roman power." Ellen White, *Testimonies for the Church,* 5:451. It is that combination of American Protestant churches that initiates the relationship with Rome. In so doing, even the citizens of the US will be influenced to demand and welcome with open arms this child of the papacy:

> "Political corruption is destroying love of justice and regard for truth; and even in free America, rulers and legislators, in order to secure *public favor*, will yield to the popular demand for a law enforcing Sunday observance."[58]

Since the apostate Protestant religious powers and the citizenry agitate for the image to the beast, Rome evidently does not assault them. So what exactly does Rome invade? Is it perhaps the civil or judicial power of the USA?

Inspiration tells us that:

> "As America, the land of religious liberty, *shall unite* with the papacy in forcing the conscience and compelling men to honor the false sabbath, the people of every country on the globe will be led to follow her example."[59]

> "The nation [America] will be on the side of the great rebel leader."[60]

When the two apostates—church and state—"shall unite" "in forcing the conscience and compelling men to honor the false Sabbath" (for only the state has the means to force and compel humanity), does that unity of purpose reflect a military assault

---

57 Ellen White, *Spalding and Magan's Unpublished Manuscript Testimonies,* 2, emphasis added.

58 Ellen White, *Great Controversy,* 592.

59 Ellen White, *Testimonies for the Church,* 6:18.

60 Ellen White, *Testimonies for the Church,* 5:136.

upon or act of aggression toward the civil government of the USA by Rome, as the prophecy demands? No. To the contrary, all three entities are seen as working in perfect union with one another.

Would Jesus, knowing beforehand the end from the beginning (See SDABC, 6:1082), inspire Daniel to use the term "glorious land" to describe the nation that has just instituted a national Sunday law with punitive consequences for those who will not concede to a false sabbath? After all, the sole event and timing of this prophecy is Rome's "entrance" at the right hand of fellowship from apostate American Protestantism. Would it not be a misleading—or even an outright false—description on heaven's part of that heaven-defying civil power that unites with Rome?

The religious, political, economic and legislative aspects of America, including her citizenry, will have been nothing but cooperative in setting up the image to the beast, making any hostility on the part of Rome unnecessary. Therefore, if Rome's attack does not come upon any of them, we are down to just two choices for the definition of the "glorious land." Either that phrase is a symbol and the assault comes upon Christ's church, as interpreted above, or the interpretation for "land" must be the literal soil of the United States that Rome is to besiege. There is nothing else left for it to mean—unless, of course, the theme of Daniel 11 is again the great controversy between Christ and Satan. In that perspective, it can readily be seen in the verses we've been discussing that Satan orchestrates his wrath through his three earthly representatives, and at their head is the bishop of Rome. The assault, then, is on Jesus Christ, through the person of His witnesses, His church:

> "He [Christ] will bring out the pattern of life and character that will be to His own glory. And that character which expresses the glory—character—of Christ will be received into the Paradise of God." Ellen White, *Desire of Ages*, 331.

We pray this examination ends the differences of opinion regarding the meanings of the two terms discussed, and leads to unity of the faith among the brethren in this particular. Especially do we hope that now any fog of confusion has been lifted, the readers see the direct and present application of the prophecy to themselves, as individual members of God's remnant church.

## DAN. 11:41…"and MANY *countries* shall be OVERTHROWN:"

Overthrown: 3782. כָּשַׁל *kāšal:* A verb meaning to stumble, to stagger, to totter, to cause to stumble, to overthrow, to make weak. This word is used literally of individuals falling or figuratively of cities and nations falling (Isa. 3:8; Hos. 14:1[2]). People can fall by the sword (Dan. 11:33); or because of evil (Prov. 24:16); wickedness (Ezek. 33:12); and iniquity (Hos. 5:5).[61]

Let it be remembered that Daniel is not delineating on minute points but giving us the big overall picture throughout these verses. This overthrowing signals the beginning of persecution for the church by the enforcement of the papal sabbath (Sunday) upon humanity. This first phase of persecution now begins with fines, imprisonment, and inducements. The word "countries" is supplied by the translators but we shall see, with the aid of Ellen White, if the "many" that are to be "overthrown" were only individuals in the USA and/or the "many" individuals of the various countries of Christendom as well? This question can be more fully understood and will be addressed after we have first defined, "Edom, and Moab, and the chief of the children of Ammon." The reader is asked to hold his or her thoughts on this issue until additional terms and concerns are defined and then its intended meaning will be revisited.

## DAN. 11:41…"but these shall ESCAPE:"

The only way to escape then out of the "hand" of the King of the North (the papacy) is to receive the seal of the living God, the seventh-day Sabbath of the fourth commandment.

## DAN. 11:41…"out of HIS HAND:"

"Hand" is a term used for power, authority, or to rule as the following scriptures confirm:

Dan. 3:17 "If it be *so*, our God whom we serve is able to deliver us from the burning fiery furnace, and he will deliver *us* out of thine "hand", O king."

---

61  Warren Baker and Eugene Carpenter, *The Complete Word Study Dictionary: Old Testament*, s.v. (Chattanooga: AMG Publishers, 2003), 529.

1 Sam. 5:11 "So they sent and gathered together all the lords of the Philistines, and said, Send away the ark of the God of Israel, and let it go again to his own place, that it slay us not, and our people: for there was a deadly destruction throughout all the city; the "hand" of God was very heavy there."

Ex. 3:20 "And I will stretch out my "hand", and smite Egypt with all my wonders which I will do in the midst thereof: and after that he will let you go."

### DAN. 11:41..."*even* EDOM, and MOAB, and the chief of the children of AMMON."

**EDOM**: "The descendants of Edom, or Esau, Jacob's older brother (Gen 36:1, 19). Because of this relationship the Edomites were recognized by the Israelites as a brother nation, and the Mosaic law provided for their admission into the Hebrew nation in the 3rd generation, whereas Moabites and Ammonites could not become full-fledged Israelites until the 10th generation (Deut 23:3–8)."[62]

**MOAB**: "1. Son of Lot's daughter by her own father (Gen 19:30–37). 2. The nation of the Moabites (mo 'a¦b§i ts), Moab's descendants. The Moabites were a brother nation of the Ammonites (Gen 19:37, 38) and both were distantly related to the Israelites, since Lot, the father of Moab, had been Abraham's nephew (ch.12:5)."[63]

**AMMON**: "The people descended from Ben-Ammi, son of Lot by his own younger daughter (Gen 19:38)."[64]

These tribes have long since disappeared for thousands of years; hence their symbolic meaning is readily apparent. Ellen

---

62  *The Seventh-day Adventist Bible Dictionary; The Seventh-day Adventist Bible Commentary,* (Hagerstown, MD: Review and Herald, 1979; 2002), 8:303.

63  The Seventh-day Adventist Bible Dictionary; *The Seventh-day Adventist Bible Dictionary; The Seventh-day Adventist Bible Commentary,* (Hagerstown, MD: Review and Herald, 1979; 2002), 8:749.

64  *The Seventh-day Adventist Bible Dictionary; The Seventh-day Adventist Bible Commentary,* (Hagerstown, MD: Review and Herald, 1979; 2002), 8:39.

White confirms the Old Testament account that these three idolatrous tribes were the enemies of God:

> "the Moabites and Ammonites, were vile, idolatrous *tribes*, rebels against God and bitter enemies of His people."[65]

> "Balaam uttered a most beautiful and sublime prophecy of the world's Redeemer and the final destruction of the enemies of God....And he closed by predicting the complete destruction of Moab and Edom...."[66]

We share the following quote from the Talmud simply for a Jewish perspective:

> **"EDOM, EDOMITES:** 3. III *the Talmud.* The Talmud regards Edom or Esau as the type of Rome, which it calls a wild boar (Seir, meaning "shaggy"), or a swine, because Hadrian had the figure of a swine placed in Jerusalem after he had rebuilt it as a pagan city. In the Middle Ages, the terms Edom and Seir were used as substitutes for Christians and Christianity (cf. Heine's poem "An Edom"); for this reason the censors always objected to these words. In *A.Z.* ioa (interpreting o*b.* 2) occurs the remarkable statement that Edom had neither writing nor language, a statement which certainly does not agree with the identification of Edom and Rome. However, it is to be taken in the sense that Edom, meaning Rome, governed its eastern provinces not by means of its own (the Latin) language and writing, but by that of the Greeks.[67]

Who then might be those three symbolic entities designated in the end of time as the enemies of God? Turning to a familiar quote in *Great Controversy* we have these words:

> "The *Protestants of the United States* will be foremost in stretching their hands across the gulf to grasp the hand of *spiritualism*; they will reach over the abyss to clasp hands with the *Roman power*; and under the influence of this threefold union,

---

65  Ellen White, *Patriarchs and Prophets*, 168.

66  Ellen White, *Patriarchs and Prophets*, 451.

67  *The Universal Jewish Encyclopedia,* "Edom" (N.Y. 1941). 3:628.

*this country* will follow in the steps of Rome in trampling on the rights of conscience."[68]

The reader will notice that Ellen White in this passage declares that the "Protestants of the United States," "spiritualism," and the "Roman power" (the papacy) do indeed make up "a" threefold union, with "this country," (America) the civil aspect, (now a fourfold union) following in the steps of Rome in trampling on the rights of conscience. But this is not "the" threefold union as depicted in Rev. 16:13:

> "I saw three unclean spirits like frogs come out of the mouth of the dragon and out of the mouth of the beast and out of the mouth of the false prophet." Rev.16:13.

The careful reader will notice that nowhere did Ellen White mention the "dragon" nor even so much as imply that she is referring to Rev. 16:13 in *Great Controversy,* 588. Unfortunately it has just been assumed by many that the "dragon" represents spiritualism. While it is agreed that the "beast" represents the papacy, and the "false prophet" represents apostate Protestantism it is the interpretation of the "dragon" that is called into question. Without a proper Biblical interpretation and assessment here we will never be able to answer our fundamental question of who "Edom," "Moab," and "Ammon" symbolically represent in Daniel 11:41. It is imperative then to define those terms with the scriptures, however, we believe the readership of this thesis is united that the first "beast" of Rev. 13 represents the papacy, thus clearly identifying the "beast" of Rev. 16:13 as one and the same. In identifying the "false prophet" we find harmony as well in that he represents "apostate Protestantism." The "false prophet" is clearly ecclesiastical in nature, a religious entity. He pretends to speak for and represent God but he speaketh a lie. It is interesting to see the close connection of Edom and Moab and Balaam in Numbers 22–24, the "false prophet" unwittingly declaring their final destruction:

---

68 Ellen White, *Great Controversy,* 588.

"the final destruction of the enemies of God....And he closed by predicting the complete destruction of Moab and Edom...."[69]

At one time the Protestant churches were without question God's spokesmen but since the summer of 1844 and their consistent rejection of truth they are no longer God's spokesmen, yet they still claim to be as such. The "false prophet" of Rev. 19:20 and the "image to the beast" of Rev. 13:12–17 have been shown by others as well (Austin P. Cooke, with much appreciation for his many insights.) to be one and the same. This is fulfilled only in apostate Protestantism:

| Revelation 13 | Revelation 19 |
| --- | --- |
| V12 He causes them…to worship the first beast (the Papacy). | V19 He is 'with the beast' (The Papacy). |
| V14 'Miracles he did in sight of the beast' (Papacy). | V14 'Worked miracles in sight of the beast' (Papacy). |
| V14 He deceives by the miracles which he did…causes all to receive a mark. (V16). | V19 'By which he deceived them who received the mark of beast.' |
| V14 To make an image to the beast. | V19 'Those who worshipped his image.' |

In defining the "dragon" we believe all are agreed that it primarily represents Satan:

Rev. 12:9 "And the great dragon was cast out, that old serpent, called the Devil, and Satan, which deceiveth the whole world: he was cast out into the earth, and his angels were cast out with him."

However the "dragon" has a secondary application as well:

Rev. 12:3 "And there appeared another wonder in heaven; and behold a great red dragon, having seven heads and ten horns, and seven crowns upon his heads."

---

69  Ellen White, *Patriarchs and Prophets*, 451.

Rev. 12:4 "And his tail drew the third part of the stars of heaven, and did cast them to the earth: and the dragon stood before the woman which was ready to be delivered, for to devour her child as soon as it was born."

Rev. 12:5 "And she brought forth a man child, who was to rule all nations with a rod of iron: and her child was caught up unto God, and *to* his throne."

Certainly the great red dragon was Satan that sought to destroy the man child but what kingdom did Satan work through to accomplish this end? We were told Satan works through "a great red dragon having seven heads and ten horns." Notice the seven crowns were upon his heads, meaning the heads are ruling. The seven heads represent the seven main kingdoms Satan has skillfully used throughout human history to accomplish his greatest objectives. In prophecy a beast represents a political power according to Dan. 7:17 and therefore the dragon, which is a beast, must represent political powers that are used by Satan to oppose the cause of God. These "heads" rule successively, one after the other, while the ten horns are contemporaries; they all reign at the same time. Who then was the ruling "head" that sought to devour the Christ child as soon as it was born?:

"The line of prophecy in which these symbols are found begins with Revelation 12, with the dragon that sought to destroy Christ at His birth. The dragon is said to be Satan (Revelation 12:9); he it was that moved upon Herod to put the Saviour to death. But the chief agent of Satan in making war upon Christ and His people during the first centuries of the Christian Era was the Roman Empire, in which paganism was the prevailing religion. *Thus while the dragon, primarily, represents Satan, it is, in a secondary sense, a symbol of pagan Rome.*"[70]

It was pagan Rome and it is pagan Rome again that is represented as a "dragon" in Bible prophecy. The same can be illustrated for the following as well:

Rev. 12:14 "And to the woman were given two wings of a great eagle, that she might fly into the wilderness, into her

---

70  *Great Controversy*, 438.

place, where she is nourished for a time, and times, and half a time, from the face of the serpent."

> Rev. 12:15 "And the serpent cast out of his mouth water as a flood after the woman, that he might cause her to be carried away of the flood."

> Rev. 12:16 "And the earth helped the woman, and the earth opened her mouth, and swallowed up the flood which the dragon cast out of his mouth."

In these verses we have the papacy designated as the "dragon." Some may inquire, is not the papacy a church?" How then can we justify the present application? The papacy is not a church; it is a political entity with a religious veneer, that "diverse" entity as described in Dan. 7:24. In Rev. 12:17 the "dragon" is representing all the professed Christian political powers at the very end of time as we will soon show. Again:

> Eze. 29:3 "Speak, and say, Thus saith the Lord GOD; Behold, I *am* against thee, Pharaoh king of Egypt, the great dragon that lieth in the midst of his rivers, which hath said, My river *is* mine own, and I have made *it* for myself."

Here we see Egypt is designated as the "dragon." Clearly then the Bible is united in its expression of this prophetic symbol. Our next question should be, "Is Ellen White in agreement with the rule of faith?" Yes:

> "*Kings* and *rulers* and *governors* have placed upon themselves the brand of antichrist, and are *represented as the dragon* who goes to make war with the saints—with those who keep the commandments of God and who have the faith of Jesus."[71]

> "In the book of Revelation under the symbols of a great red dragon, a leopard-like beast, and a beast with lamb-like horns, are brought to view, those earthly governments which are especially engaged in trampling upon God's law, and persecuting His people."[72]

---

71  Ellen White, *Testimonies to Ministers*, 39.

72  Ellen White, *Great Controversy*, 276, 1886 edition.

Therefore the "dragon" here, represents, Kings, rulers, and governors, the civil or the state who "have placed upon themselves the brand of Antichrist," that is, the papacy. Now that we are in one accord let us return to analyze Rev. 16:13:

> "I saw three unclean spirits like frogs come out of the mouth of the dragon and out of the mouth of the beast and out of the mouth of the false prophet." Rev.16:13.

According to this prediction we see that the three unclean spirits must first take possession of these three earthly entities which to the spiritually discerned is fully underway today and in turn these three entities will be used of Satan to unite the rest of the world with the papacy as its earthly leader. To say that the "dragon" represents spiritualism in this verse is thereby saying that spiritualism is to come out of the mouth of spiritualism. This is intellectually offensive for it makes no sense and must be rejected. We have previously shown under the clause when the King of the North "enters into the glorious land" that he does so from the right hand of fellowship from apostate Protestantism, Ellen White, *Testimonies for the Church,* 5:451. This in turn unites apostate Protestantism with Romanism and together the two of them demand to be heard from Caesar:

> "Political corruption is destroying love of justice and regard for truth; and even in free America, rulers and legislators, in order to secure *public favor*, will yield to the popular demand for a law enforcing Sunday observance."[73]

The state complies with the wishes of the then one mega church:

> "As America, the land of religious liberty, *shall unite* with the papacy in forcing the conscience and compelling men to honor the false sabbath, the people of every country on the globe will be led to follow her example."[74]

In this picture we have three earthly entities united in one cause by the agency of spiritualism. Spiritualism is simply the

---

73 Ellen White, *Great Controversy*, 592.

74 Ellen White, *Testimonies for the Church,* 6:18.

glue that binds the three together. The state is the much needed entity of apostate Protestantism and Romanism for without this the church has no power to enforce her dogmas and to compel the conscience. This has been forcefully brought to the front by Ellen White when she declared that the great red dragon was a beast with *lamb-like horns* as well. Ellen White, *Great Controversy*, 276, 1886 edition. This all too clearly reveals that when the King of the North "enters into the glorious land" the realm of the church, she is not alone, no; she does so with the previously described union of apostate Protestantism and the state or civil power. Therefore the three tribes or entities described by Daniel in 11:41 symbolically representing "Edom," "Moab," and "Ammon," "the enemies of God," are one and the same as described by John in Rev. 16:13 supported by the previously given details, but now Daniel is given the view and reaction from the flipside of those individuals opposed to the intrusion of the King of the North from the company of those same three entities or tribes. This reveals that when the King of the North, the papacy, "enters into the glorious land," the realm of the church, with the support of apostate Protestantism and the backing of the state that not all will be in his train. As those three entities or tribes go forth to conquer we have been told that from its commencement to the close of probation there will be a coming out from among those same three entities, or tribes, faithful souls, joining the bloodstained banner of Prince Immanuel as well. This is exactly the picture that Daniel is painting for us. A major concern for Daniel was the plight of the people of God under their various persecutors. This is forcefully portrayed by Daniel again when he says, "these shall escape out of his hand, even Edom, and Moab, and the chief of the children of Ammon." Dan. 11:41. Isaiah supports this premise as well:

Isa. 11:10 "And in that day there shall be a root of Jesse, which shall stand for an <u>ensign</u> [the seventh-day Sabbath] of the people; to it shall <u>the Gentiles seek</u>: and his rest shall be <u>glorious</u>."

Isa. 11:11 "And it shall come to pass in that day, *that* the Lord shall set his hand again the second time to recover the remnant of his people, which shall be left, from Assyria, and from Egypt, and from Pathros, and from Cush, and from Elam, and from Shinar, and from Hamath, and from the islands of the sea."

Isa. 11:12 "And he shall set up an ensign for the nations, and shall assemble the outcasts of Israel, and gather together the dispersed of Judah from the four corners of the earth."

Isa. 11:13 "The envy also of Ephraim shall depart, and the adversaries of Judah shall be cut off: Ephraim shall not envy Judah, and Judah shall not vex Ephraim."

Isa. 11:14 "But they shall fly upon the shoulders of the Philistines toward the west; they shall spoil them of the east together: <u>they shall lay their hand upon Edom and Moab; and the children of Ammon shall obey them</u>."

Isa. 11:15 "And the LORD shall utterly destroy the tongue of the Egyptian sea; and with his mighty wind shall he shake his hand over the river, and shall smite it in the seven streams, and make *men* go over dryshod."

Isa. 11:16 "<u>And there shall be an highway for the remnant of his people</u>, which shall be left, from Assyria; like as it was to Israel in the day that he came up out of the land of Egypt."

Inspiration adds the following:

"In vision I saw two armies in terrible conflict. One army was led by banners bearing the world's insignia; the other was led by the bloodstained banner of Prince Immanuel. Standard after standard was left to trail in the dust as company after company from the Lord's army joined the foe and *tribe after tribe from the ranks of the enemy united with the commandment-keeping people of God.* An angel flying in the midst of heaven put the standard of Immanuel into many hands, while a mighty general cried out with a loud voice: "Come into line. Let those who are loyal to the commandments of God and the testimony of Christ now take their position. Come out from among them, and be ye separate, and touch not the unclean, and I will receive you, and will be a Father unto you, and ye shall be My sons and daughters. Let all who will come up to the help of the Lord, to the help of the Lord against the mighty."[75]

## DAN. 11:41…"the CHIEF of the children of AMMON."

Chief:7225. ראשׁית *rē,šiyṭ*: A noun meaning the beginning, the first, the chief, the best, the firstfruits. Occurring fifty-one times in the Old Testament.…[76]

In determining the correct identity for the noun "Chief"[7225] (*rē,šiyṭ*), the context reminds us that we are dealing with a humanity seeking refuge from the assault of the King of the North. In fact the obvious reading of the text also suggests that there are to be leaders of Ammon who are to escape as well. We will develop this thought as we proceed. While the scriptures are extremely sparse here we shall view some indirect statements from Inspiration to see if "Chief" may have been commonly used in O.T. times for a leader or leaders of various tribes:

> "The royal letters to the governors of the provinces along his route, secured to Nehemiah an honorable reception and prompt assistance. And no enemy dared molest the official who was guarded by the power of the Persian king and treated with marked consideration by the provincial rulers. Nehemiah's journey was safe and prosperous. His arrival at Jerusalem, however, with the attendance of a military guard, showing that he had come on some important mission, excited the jealousy and hatred of the enemies of Israel. The heathen tribes settled near Jerusalem had previously indulged their enmity against the Jews by heaping upon them every insult and injury which they dared inflict. Foremost in this evil work were certain *chiefs of these tribes*, Sanballat the Horonite, *Tobiah the Ammonite*, and Geshem the Arabian; and from this time these leaders watched with jealous eye the movements of Nehemiah, and endeavored by every means in their power to thwart his plans and hinder his work."[77]

---

75  Ellen White, *Testimonies for the Church*, 8:41.

76  Warren Baker and Eugene Carpenter, *The Complete Word Study Dictionary: Old Testament*, s.v. (Chattanooga: AMG Publishers, 2003), 1027.

77  Ellen White, *Southern Watchman*, March 22, 1904.

"Then the *chief of the fathers and princes of the tribes of Israel*, and the captains of thousands and of hundreds, with the rulers of the king's work....[78]

"The thing which thou hast spoken is good for us to do. So I took the *chief of your tribes, wise men, and known*, and made them heads over you, captains over thousands, and captains over hundreds, and captains over fifties, and captains over tens, and officers among your tribes."[79]

"There was a ready response from the assembly. "The *chief of the fathers and princes of the tribes* of Israel, and the captains of thousands and of hundreds, with the rulers of the king's work, offered willingly, and gave for the service of the house of God of gold five thousand talents and ten thousand drams, and of silver ten thousand talents, and of brass eighteen thousand talents, and one hundred thousand talents of iron."[80]

Mat. 24:30 "And then shall appear the sign of the Son of man in heaven: and then shall all the tribes of the earth mourn, and they shall see the Son of man coming in the clouds of heaven with power and great glory."

What is hereby established is that Ellen White does confirm the suggested use of the term as valid as the obvious reading of the text demands, "the "leaders"[7225] of the children of Ammon." Dan. 11:41.

The following statement from the pen of Ellen White is a suggested application for the clause in Dan. 11:41, "the "leaders"[7225] of the children of Ammon," that shall "escape":

"While many of our *rulers* are active agents of Satan, God also has His agents among the *leading men of the nation*. The enemy moves upon his servants to propose measures that would greatly impede the work of God; but *statesmen* who fear the Lord are influenced by holy angels to oppose such propositions with unanswerable arguments. Thus a few men will hold in check a powerful current of evil. The opposition of the enemies

---

78  Ellen White, *Review and Herald*, December 11, 1888.

79  Ellen White, *Review and Herald*, December 31, 1903.

80  Ellen White, *Review and Herald*, August 24, 1905.

of truth will be restrained that the third angel's message may do its work. When the *final warning shall be given*, it will arrest the attention of these *leading men* through whom the Lord is now working, and *some of them will accept it, and will stand with the people of God through the time of trouble.*[81]

The "final warning" which is the loud cry of Rev. 18:1–5 is not given until we come to verse 44.

### DAN. 11:41..."and MANY *countries* shall be OVERTHROWN:"

Returning to a clause and question left unanswered from verse 41 and promised to be addressed after we were to have first defined, "Edom, and Moab, and the chief of the children of Ammon" will be taken up now. Were the "many" that are to be "overthrown" by the King of the North when he is to enter into the glorious land, the realm of the church, verse 41, only individuals in the USA and/or were the "many," individuals of the various countries of Christendom included as well? Our first step in identification is to correctly identify Christendom:

### Global Romanism is included in Christendom:

"The power that for so many centuries maintained despotic sway over the monarchs of Christendom is Rome."[82]

"The theory of the immortality of the soul was one of those false doctrines that Rome, borrowing from paganism, incorporated into the religion of Christendom."[83]

### Global Protestantism is included in Christendom:

"The spirit of world conforming and indifference to the testing truths for our time exists and has been gaining ground in churches of the *Protestant faith in all the countries of Christendom*; and these churches are included in the solemn and terrible

---

81   Ellen White, *Great Controversy*, 610–11.

82   Ellen White, *Great Controversy,* 382.

83   Ellen White, *The Faith I Live By*, 175.

denunciation of the second angel. But the work of apostasy has not yet reached its culmination."[84]

Now that it is established what constitutes Christendom, her occupation may not only be seen in America but Europe, South America, Africa, and any pro Catholic and Protestant countries where her presence is welcome becomes Christendom. Let us return to Rev. 16:

> Rev. 16:13 "And I saw three unclean spirits like frogs *come* out of the mouth of the dragon, and out of the mouth of the beast, and out of the mouth of the false prophet."

> Rev. 16:14 "For they are the spirits of devils, working miracles, *which* go forth unto the kings of the earth and of the whole world, to gather [unite] them to the battle of that great day of God Almighty."

When the King of the North enters into the realm of the church, first in America with his threefold union we have been told this will then divide the entire world of Christendom because the entire world of Christendom will be involved:

> "*All Christendom will be divided into two great classes*—those who keep the commandments of God and the faith of Jesus, and those who worship the beast and his image and receive his mark."[85]

> "The so-called *Christian world* is to be the theater of great and decisive actions."[86]

We now understand that the "dragon" represents, Kings, rulers, and governors that have "placed upon themselves the brand of antichrist," the papacy, (the professing Christian political powers of Christendom). However, Rev. 16:14 has shown us that there are other "Kings" and rulers and these "Kings" and rulers have not "placed upon themselves the brand of antichrist," the papacy. It logically stands that all the kingdoms represented by the dragon

---

84   Ellen White, *Great Controversy,* 389.

85   Ellen White, *Great Controversy,* 450.

86   Ellen White, *Selected Messages,* 3:392.

are the professing Christian political powers of Christendom. After all these professing powers of Christendom have "placed upon themselves the brand of antichrist," Rev. 16:14 then moves us into a new and distinct geography that we will soon illustrate to be the King of the South and the rest of the known world. Since "Egypt," the "land of Egypt" and/or the "King of the South" represents one and the same as the scriptures have already confirmed from Dan. 11:5–9. And as already illustrated, "the King of the South" and or "Egypt" the "land of Egypt" is an all-inclusive symbolic term that encompasses all organized atheistic, polytheistic and/or monotheistic kingdoms that deny the sovereignty of Christ at the end of time, confirmed in *Great Controversy*, 269 and the *Advocate*, July 1, 1899. How clear then is our meaning and identification. The same is true of Daniel 11:42 for it likewise moves us into a new and distinct geography as well, into the territory of the "land of Egypt," the king of the South and the rest of the atheistic, polytheistic and monotheists' world. These two prophecies are one and the same with Revelation giving more details. Therefore contextual evidence demonstrates that Dan. 11:41 and Rev. 16:13 are one and the same event as well, revealing a worldwide movement on the part of Christendom to place "upon themselves the brand of antichrist," the papacy, church-state entities enforcing the papal sabbath.

**Dan. 11:42 "He shall stretch forth[7971] his hand[3027] also upon the countries:[776] and the land[776] of Egypt[4714] shall not[3808] escape."[1961, 6413]**

**Dan. 11: 42…"HE shall"…**

"He," the King of the North, the papacy.

**Dan. 11: 42…"stretch forth his HAND"…**

"Hand" as we illustrated in verse 41, is a term used for power, authority, or to rule. Now that the King of the North has conquered all of professed Christendom as shown in verse 41, he confidently marches against his rival, the "land of Egypt" the King of the South. This represents the rest of the kings, rulers and peoples of the world that have not yet placed upon themselves the brand of antichrist.

## DAN. 11:42..."ALSO" ...

In Daniel 11:41 we recognized the word "also" (the Hebrew word *gam*) does not exist in the original Hebrew, the same is true of verse 42. The translators have supplied it.

## DAN. 11:42..."upon the COUNTRIES: and the land of EGYPT shall not ESCAPE."

It has already been demonstrated that Dan. 11:42 and Rev. 16:14 represent one and the same event, a united worldwide movement against the "land of Egypt" the "King of the South" on the part of Rome, the King of the North, it behooves us to take a closer look to see how his object is to be accomplished. In Rev. 16:13–14 we have five earthly entities, (1.) The "Dragon" = kings, rulers and governors, the professing Christian political powers of Christendom. (2.) The "Beast" = the papacy. (3.) The "False prophet" = apostate Protestantism. (4.) The other, "Kings" and rulers = the "King of the South," the "land of Egypt," Communism, Islam, Buddhist, etc. (5.) "And of the whole world."= the rest of the peoples comprised of the "land of Egypt". How then do these other Kings and the rest of the atheistic, polytheistic and/or monotheistic  nations such as Communism, Islam, Buddhist and the like come into line with such a wide diversity of ideologies and philosophies if they have not placed upon themselves the brand of antichrist? Rev. 16:14 tells us it will be by the means of miracles:

> "For they are the spirits of devils, working miracles, *which* go forth unto the kings of the earth and of the whole world, to gather [unite] them"...
> "The enemy is preparing to deceive the whole world by his miracle-working power."[87]

Although we cannot be definitive here this would seem to be the most logical place for the personification of Christ by Satan and other such miracles. All are agreed, it will take something of

---

87   Ellen White, Selected Messages, 2:21.

a supernatural character to unite this divisive world, the 'land of Egypt" with Christendom:

> "In this age antichrist [Satan, the real antichrist behind the King of the North] will appear as the true Christ, and *then the law of God will be fully made void in the nations of our world*. Rebellion against God's holy law *will be fully ripe*. But the true leader of all this rebellion is Satan clothed as an angel of light. Men will be deceived and will exalt him to the place of God, and deify him. But Omnipotence will interpose, and to the apostate churches that unite in the exaltation of Satan, the sentence will go forth, 'Therefore shall her plagues come in one day, death, and mourning, and famine; and she shall be utterly burned with fire: for strong is the Lord God who judgeth her.'"[88]

Let us not fail to notice that it was not until Satan appears as Christ that the law of God is then made void by the remaining nations of the world, thus fulfilling the very words of scripture in Rev. 16:14 that not even the atheistic, polytheistic and/or monotheistic nations that deny the sovereignty of Christ will escape the coming crisis. Perhaps when Satan appears as Christ he acknowledges the man of sin, the Bishop of Rome as his earthly representative and in this act the "land of Egypt" will bow to the supreme will of the papacy:

> "Rev. 13:3 "And I saw one of his heads as it were wounded to death; and his deadly wound was healed: <u>and all the world wondered after the beast</u>."

**Dan. 11:43 "But he shall have power[4910] over the treasures[4362] of gold[2091] and of silver,[3701] and over all[3605] the precious things[2530] of Egypt:[4714] and the Libyans[3864] and the Ethiopians[3569] *shall be* at his steps."[4703]**

**DAN. 11:43…"But HE"…**

"He" the King of the North, the papacy.

**DAN. 11:43…"shall have POWER"…**

"Power"[4910] (*masal*), a political term to rule, control.

---

### DAN. 11:43..."over the TREASURES of GOLD and of SILVER and over ALL the PRECIOUS things of EGYPT"...

As stated and identified in verse 40, the term "ships", according to the scriptures we have already viewed, focuses on monetary matters, which must include economy, trade, merchandise, merchants, riches, etc. Rev. 13:16–17 focuses on monetary matters as well after the image to the beast has been set up and at least some miracles have been introduced and are being displayed by supernatural agencies. Why did Daniel introduce monetary matters here? From the obvious reading of the text monetary matters seem to be well underway at the time the King of the North invades the land of Egypt, the King of the South. Is there a connection to Rev. 13:16–17? If so, does this follow the principle of repetition and enlargement? What is the role of Egypt in all of this? We believe our answer is to be found in our very next clause.

### DAN. 11:43... "and the LIBYANS and the ETHEOPIANS *shall be* at his STEPS."

The Libyans and Ethiopians are also said to "be at his steps."[4703]

Steps: "4703. מצעד *miṣ ād*: A masculine noun meaning a step, footstep....To follow a persons' steps is to imitate and adopt their actions and goals (Dan. 11:43)."[89]

When one considers the countries and conditions of Libya and Ethiopia today we rightly enquire, what could these countries possibly offer that could have any real bearing or relevance upon this prophecy today? We find little there. How then shall we identify and come to the true intended meaning for the "Libyans and the Ethiopians"? The answer is a very simple one, we must understand and identify what the "Libyans and the Ethiopians" represented to Daniel in his day. First we will begin with the scriptures:

Isa. 45:14 "Thus saith the LORD, The labour of Egypt, and merchandise of Ethiopia and of the Sabeans, men of stature,

---

89 Warren Baker and Eugene Carpenter, *The Complete Word Study Dictionary: Old Testament*, s.v. (Chattanooga: AMG Publishers, 2003), 656.

shall come over unto thee, and they shall be thine: they shall come after thee; in chains they shall come over, and they shall fall down unto thee, they shall make supplication unto thee, *saying*, Surely God *is* in thee; and *there is* none else, *there is* no God."

"The labour of Egypt, and merchandise of Ethiopia"…Who was the labor of Egypt? It was the Libyans. These people were the servant peoples to Egypt, slaves, but not in the strict sense. The Libyans were the working class or subject peoples to Egypt; many were hired as mercenaries for the Egyptian army. On the other hand, Ethiopia was the trade center of the world:

> "ETHIOPIA: The Assyrian Empire invaded Egypt in 671 B.C., driving the Ethiopian pharaohs southward and eventually sacking the Egyptian capital Thebes (biblical No-Amon; Nah.3:8) in 664 B.C. Thereafter, the realm of Ethiopian Kings was confined to Nubia, which they ruled from Napata. Ethiopia continued to be an important political force and center of trade (Isa. 45:14)."[90]

This is confirmed by the most excellent work of; A.H.L. Heeren, (1760–1842) translated from the German in 2 vols, the German historian and professor of philosophy and history at Gottingen. "Heeren's great merit as an historian was that he regarded the states of antiquity from an altogether fresh point of view. Instead of limiting himself to a narration of their political events, he exclaimed their economic relations, their constitutions, their financial systems, and thus was enabled to throw a new light on the development of the old world. He possessed vast and varied learning, perfect calmness and impartiality, and great power of historical insight, and is now looked back to as the pioneer in the movement for the economic interpretation of history."[91]

---

90 *Holman Bible Dictionary,* (Nashville Tennessee: Holman Bible Pub; 1991), 444.

91 Arnold Hermann Ludwig Heeren, *Reflections on The Politics, Intercourse, And Trade Of The Ancient Nations Of Africa—Historical Researches Into the Politics, Intercourse, and Trade Of the Carthaginians, Ethiopians And Egyptians.* (Oxford: D.A. Talboys, 1832), 1:289–479.

**DAN. 11:43…"and the LIBYANS"…**

In this prophecy we suggest that the "Libyans" represent the working class of the atheistic, polytheistic and/or monotheistic countries that will then follow in the train of the papacy.

**DAN. 11:43…"and the ETHOIPIANS"…**

In order for the papacy to have total control over all the gold, silver and precious things of Egypt, throughout the atheistic, polytheistic and/or monotheistic countries of the world, she must also control their monetary matters as well as their labor unions. This means that the papacy is to have world dominion in the old world. This is exactly what will take place:

> "*Romanism in the Old World* and apostate Protestantism in the New will pursue a similar course toward those who honor all the divine precepts."[92]

Since Russia, China, Pakistan, India, Europe and the like help make up the old world we suggest that the "Ethiopians" represent the trade center of the worlds commerce as well, under the control and jurisdiction of the papacy. A major means of controlling the commerce then will be at the support of the labor unions. This becomes transparently clear when one surveys the written directive by Ellen White on the role the labor unions will play in the last remnant of time. The second coercive device of persecution we witnessed was, "they will be forbidden to buy or sell." *Desire of Ages*, 121–122. This, in conjunction with the labor unions will first take place in America when national apostasy will be followed by national ruin. Given our global economy, it will adversely impact the entire world. **(See Appendix II, pg. 112, Labor Unions)**.

The third coercive device of persecution was that "they shall be put to death." *Desire of Ages*, 121–122. Both of these two stages will take place very close together. The third coercive device brings about the mighty shaking of the Seventh-day Adventist Church enabling the righteous then to receive the latter rain and thereby proclaim the loud cry of the fourth angel's message.

---

92  Ellen White, *Great Controversy*, 616.

The mighty shaking of the Seventh-day Adventist Church has received much speculation contrary to the plain directive of Ellen White. She thus informs us that this unfortunate process will be seen in three distinct and separate phases of which the first two have already commenced. The "first" phase:

> "God's Spirit has illuminated every page of Holy Writ, but there are those upon whom it makes little impression, because it is imperfectly understood. *When the shaking comes, by the introduction of false theories*, these surface readers, anchored nowhere, are like shifting sand. They slide into any position to suit the tenor of their feelings of bitterness…"[93]

These false theories include: heresies, miracles of healing, hypnotism, false prophets, and false shepherds among others. These poor people are unstable in all their ways and unless there is a decided change they will fail of obtaining eternal life. (See, Ellen White, *Testimonies for the Church*, 2:129–130). The "second" phase:

> "I asked the meaning of *the shaking I had seen and was shown that it would be caused by the straight testimony called forth by the counsel of the True Witness to the Laodiceans*. This will have its effect upon the heart of the receiver, and will lead him to exalt the standard and pour forth the straight truth. *Some will not bear this straight testimony*. They will rise up against it, and *this is what will cause a shaking among God's people*."[94]

This straight testimony is simply not allowing oneself to be hued and fitted for translation whether it is in following our counsel of overcoming in diet, dress, demeanor, worldliness, lust, and etc. (See, Ellen White, *Testimonies for the Church*, 1:179–195, 3:252–293, Ellen White, *Early Writings*, 269–273). However it is the third phase with which we are most concerned in our study. God has declared he is to purify his church and He will have a purified church:

> "God is sifting His people. *He will have a clean and holy church*. We cannot read the heart of man. But the Lord has provided means to keep the church pure. A corrupt people has aris-

---

93  Ellen White, *Testimonies to Ministers*, 112.

94  Ellen White, *Early Writings*, 270.

en who could not live with the people of God. They despised reproof, and would not be corrected. They had an opportunity to know that theirs was an unrighteous warfare. They had time to repent of their wrongs; but self was too dear to die. They nourished it, and it grew strong, and *they separated from the trusting people of God,* [yet they are still in the church, thus far] whom He is purifying unto Himself. We all have reason to thank God that *a way has been opened to save the church; for the wrath of God must have come upon us if these corrupt pretenders had remained with us.*

"*Every honest soul that may be deceived by these disaffected ones, will have the true light in regard to them, if every angel from heaven has to visit them, to enlighten their minds. We have nothing to fear in this matter.* As we near the judgment, [of the living] *all will manifest their true character, and it will be made plain to what company they belong.* The sieve is moving. Let us not say: Stay Thy hand, O God. The church must be purged, *and it will be.*"[95]

With such a powerful directive none can misunderstand. This cleansing or shaking of the SDA Church separates her corrupt pretenders and this will take place under the death penalty for violation of the papal sabbath. In turn, this will be shown from the following quotes to be heaven's method that purifies the church as it appears to fall; however, this separation opens the gates of heaven for the latter rain and prepares the church to proclaim the loud cry of the fourth angel. The "death penalty" constitutes the "third" phase of the shaking:

Rev. 13:15 "And he had power to give life unto the image of the beast, that the image of the beast should both speak, and cause that as many as would not worship the image of the beast should be killed."

"*When death shall be made the penalty of violating our sabbath,* [Satan speaking to his fallen angel's] then many who are now ranked with commandment keepers will come over to our side."[96]

---

95  Ellen White, *Testimonies for the Church,* 1:99–100.

96  Ellen White, *Testimonies to Ministers,* 473.

"As the storm approaches, a large class who have professed faith in the third angel's message, but have not been sanctified through obedience to the truth, abandon their position and join the ranks of the opposition. By uniting with the world and partaking of its spirit, they have come to view matters in nearly the same light; *and when the test is brought,* [The death penalty for refusing to honor the papal sabbath] they are prepared to choose the easy, popular side. Men of talent and pleasing address, who once rejoiced in the truth, employ their powers to deceive and mislead souls. They become the most bitter enemies of their former brethren. When Sabbathkeepers are brought before the courts to answer for their faith, these apostates are the most efficient agents of Satan to misrepresent and accuse them, and by false reports and insinuations to stir up the rulers against them."[97]

"The church may appear as about to fall, but it does not fall. It remains, while the sinners in Zion will be sifted out—the chaff separated from the precious wheat. This is a terrible ordeal, but nevertheless it must take place."[98]

"*The shaking of God* blows away multitudes like dry leaves. Prosperity multiplies a mass of professors. Adversity purges them out of the church."[99]

"Laws enforcing the observance of Sunday as the Sabbath will bring about a national apostasy from the principles of republicanism upon which the government has been founded. The religion of the Papacy will be accepted by the rulers, and the law of God will be made void.

When the *fifth seal was opened,* John the Revelator in vision saw *beneath the altar the company that were slain for the Word of God* and the testimony of Jesus Christ. [The death penalty for those who still refuse to honor the papal sabbath.] *After this came the scenes described in the eighteenth of Revelation,* when those who are faithful and true are called out from Babylon." [Revelation 18:1–5, quoted.][100]

---

97  Ellen White, *Great Controversy*, 608.

98  Ellen White, *Selected Messages*, 2:380.

99  Ellen White, *Testimonies for the Church*, 4:89.

100 Ellen White, *Manuscript Releases*, 20:14.

*"Mystic Babylon has not been sparing in the blood of the saints* and shall we [not] be wide awake to catch the beams of light which have been shining from the light of the angel who is to brighten the earth with his glory."[101]

"The Lord will work so that the disaffected ones will be separated from the true and loyal ones. Those who, like *Cornelius*, will fear God and glorify Him, will take their places. The ranks will not be diminished. Those who are firm and true will close up the *vacancies* that are made by those who become *offended and apostatize*."[102]

"And because iniquity shall abound, the love of many shall wax cold." The very atmosphere is polluted with sin. Soon God's people will be tested by fiery trials, and the great proportion of those who now appear to be genuine and true will prove to be base metal. Instead of being strengthened and confirmed by opposition, threats, and abuse, they will cowardly take the side of the opposers. The promise is: "Them that honor Me I will honor." Shall we be less firmly attached to God's law because the world at large have attempted to make it void?

Already the judgments of God are abroad in the land, as seen in storms, in floods, in tempests, in earthquakes, in peril by land and by sea. The great I AM is speaking to those who make void His law. When God's wrath is poured out upon the earth, who will then be able to stand? Now is the time for God's people to show themselves true to principle. When the religion of Christ is most held in contempt, when His law is most despised, then should our zeal be the warmest and our courage and firmness the most unflinching. To stand in defense of truth and righteousness when the majority forsake us, to fight the battles of the Lord when champions are few—this will be our test. At this time we must gather warmth from the coldness of others, courage from their cowardice, and loyalty from their treason. The nation will be on the side of the great rebel leader.[103]

"But the days of purification of the church are hastening on apace. God will have a people pure and true. In the mighty sifting soon to take place we shall be better able to measure the

---

101 Ellen White, *Letter*, 112, 1890. *Selected Messages*, 3:426.

102 Ellen White, *Ms 97*, 1898, p. 6. *Manuscript Releases*, 2:57.

103 Ellen White, *Testimonies for the Church*, 5:136.

strength of Israel. The signs reveal that the time is near when the Lord will manifest that His fan is in His hand, and He will thoroughly purge His floor."[104]

"Coldness and contempt may be harder to endure than martyrdom...." [105]

"*Before giving us the baptism of the Holy Spirit*, our heavenly Father will *try us*, to see if we can live without dishonoring Him [by not bowing down to the death decree].... Do not think that you can have great spiritual blessings [the latter rain] without complying with the conditions God Himself has laid down."[106]

"As we near the close of this earth's history, we advance more and more rapidly in Christian growth, or we retrograde just as decidedly."[107]

Isa. 57:1 "The righteous perisheth, and no man layeth *it* to heart: and merciful men *are* taken away, none considering that the righteous is taken away from the evil *to come*."

**Dan. 11:44 "But tidings[8052] out of the east[4480, 4217] and out of the north[4480, 6828] shall trouble[926] him: therefore he shall go forth[3318] with great[1419] fury[2534] to destroy,[8045] and utterly to make away[2763] many."[7227]**

**DAN. 11:44..."But TIDINGS"...**

"Tidings"[8052] this represents the announcement of a prophetic message, the angel of Rev. 18:1–5.

"8052. שמועה *šᵉmû âh:* A feminine noun referring to a report; news; a rumor. Literally, it means what is heard, a passive participle from *šâmaʿ,* to hear, to understand. It refers to a report or announcement of news, a report of something, even a rumor (1 Sam. 2:24; 4:19; 2 Sam. 4:4; 13:30). Daniel uses the

---

104 Ellen White, *Testimonies for the Church,* 5:80.
105 Ellen White, Letter 30a, 1892.
106 Ellen White, *Letter,* 22, 1902. *Manuscript Releases,* 4:336.
107 Ellen White, *Letter,* 1f, 1890.

plural form of the word, rumors (Dan. 11:44). It indicates what is heard by a prophet, the message, the prophesy (Isa. 28:9, 19; 53:1); what is heard (Obad. 1:1)."[108]

"When do her sins reach unto heaven [Revelation 18:2–5]? When the law of God is finally made void by legislation."[109]

"The so-called Christian world is to be the theater of great and decisive actions. Men in authority will enact laws controlling the conscience, after the example of the papacy. Babylon will make all nations drink of the wine of the wrath of her fornication. Every nation will be involved. Of this time, John the Revelator declares: [Revelation 18:3–7, quoted]."

"These have one mind, and shall give their power and strength unto the beast. These shall make war with the Lamb, and the Lamb shall overcome them: for He is Lord of lords, and King of kings: and they that are with Him are called, and chosen, and faithful." [Revelation 17:13, 14].

"These have one mind." There will be a universal bond of union, one great harmony, a confederacy of Satan's forces. "And shall give their power and strength unto the beast." Thus is manifested the same arbitrary, oppressive power against religious liberty, freedom to worship God according to the dictates of conscience, as was manifested by the papacy, when in the past it persecuted those who dared to refuse to conform with the religious rites and ceremonies of Romanism."[110]

The angel of Rev. 18 that comes down and lightens the whole earth with his glory is equated by Ellen White with the outpouring of the latter rain:

"Then let us show it by our works, and remove from our hearts everything that will shut out Jesus. The latter rain is to fall upon the people of God. A mighty angel is to come down

---

108 Warren Baker and Eugene Carpenter, *The Complete Word Study Dictionary: Old Testament,* (Chattanooga, TN: AMG Publishers 2003), 1160.

109 Ellen G. White, *Signs of the Times,* June 12, 1893.

110 Ellen White, *Manuscript Releases,* 19:242.

from heaven, and the whole earth is to be lighted with his glo-ry."[111]

"Every truly converted soul will be intensely desirous to bring others from the darkness of error into the marvelous light of the righteousness of Jesus Christ. The great outpouring of the Spirit of God, which lightens the whole earth with his glory, will not come until we have an enlightened people, that know by experience what it means to be laborers together with God."[112]

"Those who follow in the light need have no anxiety lest that in the outpouring of the latter rain they will not be baptized with the Holy Spirit. If we would receive the light of the glori-ous angel that shall lighten the earth with his glory, let us see to it that our hearts are cleansed, emptied of self, and turned toward heaven, that they may be ready for the latter rain. Let us be obtaining a fitting up to join in the proclamation of the angel who shall lighten the earth with his glory."[113]

## DAN. 11:44…"out of the EAST"…

What message do the scriptures point to in the last remnant of time under the power of the fourth angel that comes from the east? The "sealing" message:

Rev. 7:1 "And after these things I saw four angels standing on the four corners of the earth, holding the four winds of the earth, that the wind should not blow on the earth, nor on the sea, nor on any tree."

Rev. 7:2 "And I saw another angel ascending from the east, having the seal of the living God: and he cried with a loud voice to the four angels, to whom it was given to hurt the earth and the sea,"

Rev. 7:3 "Saying, Hurt not the earth, neither the sea, nor the trees, till we have sealed the servants of our God in their foreheads."

---

111  Ellen White, *Review and Herald*, April 21, 1891.

112  Ellen White, *Review and Herald*, July 21, 1896.

113  Ellen White, *Signs of the Times*, August 1, 1892.

Rev. 7:4 "And I heard the number of them which were sealed: and there were sealed an hundred and forty and four thousand of all the tribes of the children of Israel."

"The sealing is a pledge from God of perfect security to His chosen ones (Exodus 31:13–17). Sealing indicates you are God's chosen. He has appropriated you to Himself. As the sealed of God we are Christ's purchased possession, and no one shall pluck us out of His hands."[114]

To understand the sealing aright it must be viewed in its three separate and distinct phases in the plan of salvation. The "first" phase or seal is introduced in the book of Ephesians. This seal or sealing is administered at conversion:

Eph. 1:13 "In whom ye also *trusted*, after that ye heard the word of truth, the gospel of your salvation: in whom also after that ye believed, ye were sealed with that holy Spirit of promise,"

Eph. 1:14 "Which is the earnest of our inheritance until the redemption of the purchased possession, unto the praise of his glory."

Eph. 4:30 "And grieve not the holy Spirit of God, whereby ye are sealed unto the day of redemption."

The "second" phase of the seal or sealing of the born again Christian is administered when he or she accepts the Biblical Sabbath:

Isa. 8:16 "Bind up the testimony, seal the law among my disciples."

The "seal of the law" is found in none other than the Sabbath of the fourth commandment. This is confirmed from the following:

"*The Sabbath* will be the great test of loyalty, for it is the point of truth especially controverted. When the final test shall be brought to bear upon men, then the line of distinction will be drawn between those who serve God and those who serve Him

---

114 Ellen White, *Manuscript Releases*, 15:225.

not. While the observance of the false sabbath in compliance with the law of the state, contrary to the fourth commandment, will be an avowal of allegiance to a power that is in opposition to God, the keeping of the true Sabbath, in obedience to God's law, is an evidence of loyalty to the Creator. While one class, by accepting the sign of submission to earthly powers, receive the mark of the beast, the other choosing the token of allegiance to divine authority, *receive the seal of God*."[115]

The "third" phase of the seal or sealing is what Ellen White calls the seal of protection (*Early Writings*, 71) that all must have to be shielded during the time of trouble, the seven last plagues. This seal or sealing is found in Ezekiel:

Eze. 9:1 "He cried also in mine ears with a loud voice, saying, Cause them that have charge over the city to draw near, even every man *with* his destroying weapon in his hand."

Eze. 9:2 "And, behold, six men came from the way of the higher gate, which lieth toward the north, and every man a slaughter weapon in his hand; and one man among them *was* clothed with linen, with a writer's inkhorn by his side: and they went in, and stood beside the brasen altar."

Eze. 9:3 "And the glory of the God of Israel was gone up from the cherub, whereupon he was, to the threshold of the house. And he called to the man clothed with linen, which *had* the writer's inkhorn by his side;"

Eze. 9:4 "And the LORD said unto him, Go through the midst of the city, through the midst of Jerusalem, and set a mark upon the foreheads of the men that sigh and that cry for all the abominations that be done in the midst thereof."

Eze. 9:5 "And to the others he said in mine hearing, Go ye after him through the city, and smite: let not your eye spare, neither have ye pity:"

Eze. 9:6 "Slay utterly old *and* young, both maids, and little children, and women: but come not near any man upon whom

---

115 Ellen White, *Great Controversy*, 605.

*is* the mark; and begin at my sanctuary. Then they began at the ancient men which *were* before the house."

This sealing of Ezekiel 9:1–6 and Rev. 7:1–4 is vividly portrayed by Ellen White as one and the same event:

"If such scenes as this are to come, such tremendous judgments on a guilty world, where will be the refuge for God's people? *How will they be sheltered until the indignation be overpast?* John sees the elements of nature—earthquake, tempest, and political strife—represented as being held by four angels. These winds are under control until God gives the word to let them go. There is the safety of God's church. The angels of God do His bidding, holding back the winds of the earth, that the winds should not blow on the earth, nor on the sea, nor on any tree, until the servants of God should be sealed in their foreheads. The mighty angel is seen ascending from the east (or sunrising). This mightiest of angels has in his hand the seal of the living God, or of Him who alone can give life, who can inscribe upon the foreheads the mark or inscription, to whom shall be granted immortality, eternal life. It is the voice of this highest angel that had authority to command the four angels to keep in check the four winds until this work was performed, and until he should give the summons to let them loose. Those that overcome the world, the flesh, and the devil, will be the favored ones who shall receive the seal of the living God. Those whose hands are not clean, whose hearts are not pure, will not have the seal of the living God. Those who are planning sin and acting it will be passed by. Only those who, in their attitude before God, are filling the position of those who are repenting and confessing their sins in the great anti-typical day of atonement, will be recognized and marked as worthy of God's protection. The names of those who are steadfastly looking and waiting and watching for the appearing of their Saviour—more earnestly and wishfully than they who wait for the morning—will be numbered with those who are sealed. Those who, while having all the light of truth flashing upon their souls, should have works corresponding to their avowed faith, but are allured by sin, setting up idols in their hearts, corrupting their souls before God, and polluting those who unite with them in sin, will have their names blotted out of the book of life, and be left in midnight darkness, having no oil in their vessels with their lamps. "Unto you that fear My name shall the Sun of Righteousness arise with healing in His wings."

72

This sealing of the servants of God is the same that was shown to Ezekiel in vision. John also had been a witness of this most startling revelation."[116]

This will be a time of severe trial for God's people as the faithful (from laity to leadership) must sigh and cry for all the abominations that are being done in the land and from those who have apostatized from the church.

"Light must come to the people through agents whom God shall choose, who will give the note of warning, that none may be in ignorance of the purposes of God or the devices of Satan. At the great heart of the work, Satan will use his hellish arts to the utmost. He will seek in every possible way to interpose himself between the people and God, and shut away the light that God would have come to his children. It is his design to keep them in ignorance of what shall come upon the earth. All should be prepared to hear the signal trumpet of the watchman, and be ready to pass the word along the walls of Zion, that the people may prepare themselves for the conflict. The people must not be left to stumble their way along in darkness, not knowing what is before them, and unprepared for the great issues that are coming."[117]

When in the chain of events does this sealing take place? It takes place *after* the latter rain, *after* the loud cry of Rev. 18:1–5 when the third angel's message is closing, just before the close of probation, just before the falling of the seven last plagues:

"Servants of God, endowed with power from on high with their faces lighted up, and shining with holy consecration, [having received the latter rain, represented as "their faces lighted up"] went forth to proclaim the message [Rev. 18:1–5] from heaven. Souls that were scattered all through the religious bodies answered to the call, and the precious were hurried out of the doomed churches, as Lot was hurried out of Sodom before her destruction. God's people were strengthened by the excellent glory which rested upon them in rich abundance and prepared them to endure the hour of temptation. I heard everywhere a

---

116 Ellen White, *Testimonies to Ministers*, 444–5.

117 Ellen White, *Review and Herald*, December 24, 1889. See also, *Ezekiel* 8:1–11:2; Ellen White, *Testimonies for the Church*, 5:207–216.

multitude of voices saying, "Here is the patience of the saints: here are they that keep the commandments of God, and the faith of Jesus."

I was pointed down to the time when the third angel's message was *closing*. The power of God *had* rested upon His people; they *had* accomplished their work and were prepared for the trying hour before them. They *had* received the latter rain, or refreshing from the presence of the Lord, and the living testimony *had* been revived. The last great warning *had* sounded everywhere, *and it had stirred up and enraged the inhabitants of the earth who would not receive the message.*

I saw angels hurrying to and fro in heaven. *An angel with a writer's inkhorn by his side returned from the earth and reported to Jesus that his work was done, and the saints were numbered and sealed.* Then I saw Jesus, who had been ministering before the ark containing the ten commandments, throw down the censer. He raised His hands, and with a loud voice said, "It is done." And all the angelic host laid off their crowns as Jesus made the solemn declaration, "He that is unjust, let him be unjust still: and he which is filthy, let him be filthy still: and he that is righteous, let him be righteous still: and he that is holy, let him be holy still."

Every case had been decided for life or death. While Jesus had been ministering in the sanctuary, the judgment had been going on for the righteous dead, and then for the righteous living. Christ had received His kingdom, having made the atonement for His people and blotted out their sins. The subjects of the kingdom were made up. The marriage of the Lamb was consummated. And the kingdom, and the greatness of the kingdom under the whole heaven, was given to Jesus and the heirs of salvation, and Jesus was to reign as King of kings and Lord of lords."[118]

This short study will also clarify for the reader when the Bible or Ellen White speak of the "sealing" the context will determine which phase heaven is alluding to.

### DAN. 11:44..."and out of the NORTH"...

Almost always without exception when ancient Israel was attacked from her enemies it came from the north:

---

118 Ellen White, *Early Writings*, 278–280.

Jer. 4:6 "Set up the standard toward Zion: retire, stay not: for I will bring evil from the "north," and a great destruction."

Jer. 6:22 "Thus saith the LORD, Behold, a people cometh from the north country, and a great nation shall be raised from the sides of the earth."

Jer. 6:23 "They shall lay hold on bow and spear; they *are* cruel, and have no mercy; their voice roareth like the sea; and they ride upon horses, set in array as men for war against thee, O daughter of Zion."

Jer. 51:48 "Then the heaven and the earth, and all that *is* therein, shall sing for Babylon: for the spoilers shall come unto her from the "north," saith the LORD."

Eze. 26:7 "For thus saith the Lord GOD; Behold, I will bring upon Tyrus Nebuchadrezzar king of Babylon, a king of kings, from the "north," with horses, and with chariots, and with horsemen, and companies, and much people."

The point not to be missed here under the loud cry of Rev. 18:1–5 is in verse four where we have the action required of those who will heed the last warning message: "Come out of her…that ye receive not of her plagues" the judgments of God, represented as coming from the "north" in the seven last plagues. That is the significance and meaning of the "tidings" or message from, "out of the north." Let it be remembered that "Mt. Zion" and "God's throne" are represented in Ps. 48:2 and Isa. 14:13 as in the "sides of the north." Rev. 15:8 declares "no man [or being] was able to enter into the "temple," till the seven plagues of the seven angels were fulfilled." The seven last plagues come from the north just as the mighty angel descends from the east with the seal of the living God.

### DAN. 11:44…"shall TROULBLE HIM:"…

"Trouble"[926] (*bâhal)* A verb meaning to be dismayed or terrified, to tremble inwardly or to be suddenly alarmed or enraged, that is, the King of the North, the papacy.

**DAN. 11:44…"therefore HE"…**

"He," the papacy.

**DAN. 11:44…"shall go forth with GREAT FURY to DESTROY and UTTERLY to MAKE AWAY MANY."**

This foretells that many of God's people will also be martyred under the empowerment of the latter rain in proclaiming the loud cry. This is the response from the King of the North and the world at large from the loud cry of Rev. 18:

> "The last great warning had sounded everywhere, [Rev. 18:1–5] and it had stirred up and *enraged the inhabitants of the earth who would not receive the message.*"[119]

We have been amply warned of what we are to encounter under the loud cry:

> Rev. 20:4 "And I saw thrones, and they sat upon them, and judgment was given unto them: and *I saw* the souls of them that were beheaded for the witness of Jesus, and for the word of God, and which had not worshipped the beast, neither his image, neither had received *his* mark upon their foreheads, or in their hands; and they lived and reigned with Christ a thousand years."
>
> "Christ warned his disciples in regard to what they would meet in their work as evangelists. He knew what their sufferings would be, what trials and hardships they would be called upon to bear. He would not hide from them the knowledge of what they would have to encounter, lest trouble, coming unexpectedly, should shake their faith. 'I have told you before it come to pass,' he said, 'that, when it is come to pass, ye might believe.' Their faith was to be strengthened, rather than weakened, by the coming of trial. They would say to one another, "He told us that this would come, and what we must do to meet it."[120]

> "We have a living Saviour, and he has not left us in the world to fight the battles alone. No, but He has not flattered us (either)…. He tells us…. "that whosoever killeth you will think that he doeth God service" (John 16:12)

---

119 Ellen White, *Early Writings*, 279.

120 Ellen White, *Review and Herald*, April 20, 1911.

This is a terrible deception that comes upon the human mind. *But here He has shown you the plan of the battle. He tells you what you are to meet*: "We wrestle not against flesh and blood, but against principalities, against powers, against the rulers of the darkness of this world, against wickedness in high places" (Ephesians 6:12)[121]

"At the *eleventh hour* the Lord will call into his service many faithful workers. Self-sacrificing men and women will step into the places made *vacant by apostasy and death*. To *young men* and *young women*, as well as to those who are *older*, God will give power from above. With converted minds, converted hands, converted feet, and converted tongues, *their lips touched with a living coal from the divine altar*, they will go forth into the Master's service, moving steadily onward and upward, *carrying the work forward to completion*."[122]

"We need not be surprised at anything that may take place now. We need not marvel at any developments of horror. Those who trample under their unholy feet the law of God have the same spirit as had the men who insulted and betrayed Jesus. Without any compunctions of conscience they will do the deeds of their father the devil."[123]

"The persecutions of Protestants by Romanism, by which the religion of Jesus Christ was almost annihilated, will be more than rivaled when Protestantism and popery are combined."[124]

"Many will fall at their post, betrayed and condemned by their fellowmen."[125]

"The two armies will stand distinct and separate, and this distinction will be so marked that many who shall be convinced of the truth will come on the side of God's commandment-keeping people. When this grand work is to take place in the battle, prior to the last closing conflict, many will be imprisoned, many

---

121 Ellen White, *Ms* 49, 1894.

122 Ellen White, *Youth Instructor*, February 13, 1902.

123 Ellen White, *Selected Messages,* 3:416.

124 Ellen White, *Selected Messages*, 3:387.

125 Ellen White, *Letter*, 230, 1907.

will flee for their lives from cities and towns, and many will be martyrs for Christ's sake in standing in defense of the truth."[126]

"How much of evil would be averted, if all, when falsely accused, would avoid recrimination, and in its stead employ mild, conciliating words."[127]

Many Jewish expositors recognize this as a universal religious boycott, not to be confused with the one issued in *Great Controversy,* 615–6, 626, 631, 635 between the second and third plagues after the close of probation.

Lest we fail to mention and be blindsided here, we must unmask a myth that declares after the latter rain has fallen there will be no more martyrdom. That supposition is totally false. In recapping *Early Writings* we were told:

"Servants of God, endowed with power from on high with their faces lighted up, and shining with holy consecration, [having received the latter rain, represented as "their faces lighted up" just like Stephen's face under the early rain] went forth to proclaim the message [Rev. 18:1–5] from heaven."[128]

Was Stephen exempt from martyrdom under the early rain? No, and as the text in Daniel under discussion, it is obvious that we who will be alive then will not be exempt as well. As we previously noted earlier in *Early Writings,* 279, the seal of protection of Rev. 7:1–4 and Eze. 9:1–6 does not take place until *after* the latter rain *after* the loud cry of Rev. 18:1–5 when the third angel's message is closing, just before the close of probation, just before the falling of the seven last plagues. It is only after the close of probation that God will not allow anymore martyrdom for this is a heaven-ordained method to vindicate the truth and convince others of the truth:

"If the blood of Christ's faithful witnesses were shed at this time, [during the seven last plagues] it would not, like the blood of the martyrs, be as seed sown to yield a harvest for God.

---

126 Ellen White, *Selected Messages,* 3:397.

127 Ellen White, *Signs of the Times,* May 12, 1881.

128 Ellen White, *Early Writings,* 278–9.

Their fidelity would not be a testimony to convince others of the truth; for the obdurate heart has beaten back the waves of mercy until they return no more. If the righteous were now left to fall a prey to their enemies, it would be a triumph for the prince of darkness."[129]

"Whenever persecution takes place, the spectators make decisions either for or against Christ."[130]

"There is no necessity for thinking that we cannot endure persecution; we shall have to go through terrible times."[131]

**Dan. 11:45 "And he shall plant[5193] the tabernacles[168] of his palace[643] between[996] the seas[3220] in the glorious[6643] holy[6944] mountain;[2022] yet he shall come[935] to[5704] his end,[7093] and none[369] shall help[5826] him."**

## DAN. 11:45..."And HE"...

"He," the papacy.

## DAN. 11:45..."And he shall PLANT"...

5193. נָטַע *nāta* : A verb meaning to plant, to establish.[132]

The papacy is not looking at "establishing" a temporary dwelling, no, "for she saith in her heart, I sit a queen, and am no widow, and shall see no sorrow." Rev. 18:7.

## DAN. 11:45..."the TABERNACLES of his PALACE"...

The papacy establishes her seat among the nations:

"Peter exclaims, "Master, it is good for us to be here: and let us make *three tabernacles*; one for Thee, and one for Moses, and one for Elias." The disciples are confident that Moses and

---

129 Ellen White, *Great Controversy*, 634.

130 Ellen White, *Review and Herald*, December 20, 1898.

131 Ellen White, *Review and Herald*, April 29, 1890.

132 Warren Baker-Eugene Carpenter, *The Complete Word Study Dictionary: Old Testament,* (Chattanooga, TN: AMG Publishers 2003), 728.

Elijah have been sent to protect their Master, *and to establish His authority as king.*"[133]

"Tabernacles" is an ecclesiastical term while "palace" is a political term. This is a union of church and state in the end of time as these scriptures likewise confirm:

> Rev. 17:1 "And there came one of the seven angels which had the seven vials, and talked with me, saying unto me, Come hither; I will shew unto thee the judgment [punishment] of the great whore that sitteth upon many waters:

> Rev. 17:2 "With whom the kings of the earth have committed fornication, and the inhabitants of the earth have been made drunk with the wine of her fornication.

> Mk. 13:9 "But take heed to yourselves: for they shall deliver you up to councils; and in the synagogues ye shall be beaten: and ye shall be brought before rulers and kings for my sake, for a testimony against them."

> Lk. 21:12 "But before all these, they shall lay their hands on you, and persecute *you*, delivering *you* up to the synagogues, and into prisons, being brought before kings and rulers for my name's sake.

## DAN. 11:45..."between the SEAS" ...

Rev. 17:15 interpret "waters" in Bible prophecy as peoples, and multitudes, and nations, and tongues. This same event is presented in Rev. 17:1:

> Rev. 17:1 "And there came one of the seven angels which had the seven vials, and talked with me, saying unto me, Come hither; I will shew the judgment[2917] [punishment] of the great whore <u>that sitteth upon many waters</u>:" (See my Exposition of Revelation chapter 17).

> **2917. κρίμα *kríma*;** gen. *krímatos*, neut. noun from *krínō* (2919), **(B)** More often a sentence of punishment or condemnation, implying also the punishment itself as a certain conse-

---

133 Ellen White, *Desire of Ages*, 422.

quence (Matt. 23:14; Mark 12:40; Luke 20:47; 23:40; 24:20; Rom. 2:2, 3; 3:8; 13:2; 1 Cor. 11:29, 34; Gal. 5:10; 1 Tim. 3:6; 5:12; James 3:1; 2 Pet. 2:3; Jude 1:4; Rev. 17:1; 18:20; Sept.: Deut. 21:22; Jer. 4:12).[134]

## DAN.11:45..."IN the GLORIOUS HOLY MOUNTAIN" ...

"In" The King of the North has from the very beginning of the conflict in verse 41 been biding her time to strike and "enter into" the remnant church and desolate her members and borders. At this stage of the conflict it appears as if the papacy has succeeded in her world conquest.

The "glorious holy mountain" has been explained previously to be the "church triumphant" her faithful members are all accounted for and Christ's Kingdom is complete, forever established at the close of probation. **(See, pgs. 36–39)**

## DAN. 11:45..."yet he shall come to his END, and none shall help him"...

End: 7093. קֵץ qēs: A masculine noun indicating an end of time or space. It refers to the finish, a final point, a goal of time, a space, or a purpose: It indicates a certain point reached in time (Gen. 4:3); the finish or demise of something, e.g., the human race (Gen. 6:13); the conclusion of a set period of time, e.g. forty days with the preposition min (4480) (Gen. 8:6; 16:3). There is an end of things, e.g., Israel (Amos 8:2). The final end of things as foretold by the prophets will be a time of the end (Ezek. 21:25[30], 29[34]; Dan. 8:17; 11:35, 40; 12:4, 9; Hab. 2:3); of God's peace in His kingdom, there will be no end (Isa. 9:7[6]); of people's life-long labor, toil, there is no cessation (Eccl. 4:8). In a spatial sense, it refers to the most remote areas (2 Kgs. 19:23; Jer. 50:26). There is seemingly no end to the flow of people, their number or extent (Eccl. 4:16). In a figurative sense, it describes the end or limit of words (Job 16:3); the completion of perfection attained in God's commandments (Ps. 119:96). The phrase miqqēs yāmim layyāmîm means at the end time of each year (2 Sam. 14:26). The word, with min (4480), followed by an infinitive of hāyāh is used to indicate the end of a set period of time (Esth. 2:12). With

---

134 Zodhiates, S; *The Complete Word Study Dictionary*: New Testament, (AMG Publishers: Chattanooga, TN, 2000), 888.

the definite article attached, it combines with the two following words to mean at the end of days of two years, that is, after two years (2 Chr. 21:19). It indicates the close of Israel's long period of oppression in Egypt, 430 years (2 Chr. 21:19)."[135]

The "end" specified here is the close of probation. (For a parallel text found in Rev. 17:12, see my Exposition of Revelation, chapter 17). Peter declares that the judgment begins with the church:

> "For the time *is come* that judgment must begin at the house of God: and if *it* first *begin* at us, what shall the end *be* of them that obey not the gospel of God?" 1Peter 4:17

In agreement with Peter, Ellen White describes the close of probation first for the Adventist Church:

> "Oh, that the people might know the time of their visitation! There are many who have not yet heard the testing truth for this time. There are many with whom the Spirit of God is striving. The time of God's destructive judgments is the time of mercy for those who have had no opportunity to learn what is truth. Tenderly will the Lord look upon them. His heart of mercy is touched; His hand is still stretched out to save, while the door is closed to those who would not enter."[136]

Ellen White now describes the close of probation for the world:

> "Jesus has left us word: "Watch ye therefore: for ye know not when the Master of the house cometh, at even, or at midnight, or at the cockcrowing, or in the morning: lest coming suddenly He find you sleeping. And what I say unto you I say unto all, Watch." We are waiting and watching for the return of the Master, who is to bring the morning, lest coming suddenly He find us sleeping. What time is here referred to? Not to the revelation of Christ in the clouds of heaven to find a people asleep. No; but to His return from His ministration in the most holy place of the heavenly sanctuary, when He lays off His

135 Warren Baker and Eugene Carpenter, *The Complete Word Study Dictionary: Old Testament*, s.v. (Chattanooga: AMG Publishers, 2003), 1004–5.

136 Ellen White, *Testimonies for the Church*, 9:97.

priestly attire and clothes Himself with garments of vengeance, and when the mandate goes forth: "He that is unjust, let him be unjust still: and he which is filthy, let him be filthy still: and he that is righteous, let him be righteous still; and he that is holy, let him be holy still."

When Jesus ceases to plead for man, the cases of all are forever decided. This is the time of reckoning with His servants. To those who have neglected the preparation of purity and holiness, which fits them to be waiting ones to welcome their Lord, the sun sets in gloom and darkness, and rises not again. Probation closes; Christ's intercessions cease in heaven. This time finally comes suddenly upon all, and those who have neglected to purify their souls by obeying the truth are found sleeping."[137]

"The world is no more ready to credit the message for this time than were the Jews to receive the Saviour's warning concerning Jerusalem. Come when it may, the day of God will come unawares to the ungodly. When life is going on in its unvarying round; when men are absorbed in pleasure, in business, in traffic, in money-making; when religious leaders are magnifying the world's progress and enlightenment, and the people are lulled in a false security—then, as the midnight thief steals within the unguarded dwelling, so shall sudden destruction come upon the careless and ungodly, and they shall not escape.' Verse 3."[138]

"But there is a day that God hath appointed for the close of this world's history. This gospel of the kingdom shall be preached in all the world for a witness unto all nations; and then shall the end come." Prophecy is fast fulfilling. More, much more, should be said about these tremendously important subjects. The day is at hand when the destiny of every soul will be fixed forever. This day of the Lord hastens on apace. The false watchmen are raising the cry, "All is well"; but the day of God is rapidly approaching. Its footsteps are so muffled that it does not arouse the world from the deathlike slumber into which it has fallen. While the watchmen cry, "Peace and safety," "sudden destruction cometh upon them," "and they shall not escape"; "for as a snare shall it come on all them that dwell on the face of

---

137 Ellen White, *Testimonies for the Church*, 2:190–1.

138 Ellen White, *Great Controversy*, 38.

the whole earth." It overtakes the pleasure-lover and the sinful man as a thief in the night. When all is apparently secure, and men retire to contented rest, then the prowling, stealthy, midnight thief steals upon his prey. When it is too late to prevent the evil, it is discovered that *some door* or window was not secured. ["When we make any reserve we are leaving open *a door* through which Satan can enter to lead us astray by his temptations." *Mount of Blessings*, 92.] "Be ye also ready: for in such an hour as ye think not the Son of man cometh." People are now settling to rest, imagining themselves secure under the popular churches; but let all beware, lest there is a place left open for the enemy to gain an entrance. Great pains should be taken to keep this subject before the people. The solemn fact is to be kept not only before the people of the world, but before our own churches also, that the day of the Lord will come suddenly, unexpectedly. The fearful warning of the prophecy is addressed to every soul. Let no one feel that he is secure from the danger of being surprised. Let no one's interpretation of prophecy rob you of the conviction of the knowledge of events which show that this great event is near at hand."[139]

The tyrannical reign of the King of the North now comes to its close and Dan. 12:1 tells us how this will be accomplished.

**Dan. 12:1 "And at that[1931] time[6256] shall Michael[4317] stand up,[5975] the great[1419] prince[8269] which standeth[5975] for[5921] the children[1121] of thy people:[5971] and there shall be[1961] a time[6256] of trouble,[6869] such as[834] never[3808] was[1961] since there was[4480, 1961] a nation[1471] even to[5704] that same[1931] time:[6256] and at that[1931] time[6256] thy people[5971] shall be delivered,[4422] every one[3605] that shall be found[4672] written[3789] in the book."[5612]**

### DAN. 12:1…"And at THAT TIME"…

The antecedent to "that time" or "in that time" a better translation, is found in Dan. 11:45, for "in that time" (the Hebrew implies a very short period of time) is in reference to when the King of the North was to "plant" his world seat among the nations having put down all opposition.

---

139 Ellen White, *Fundamentals of Christian Education*, 335–6.

## DAN. 12:1…"shall MICHAEL stand up, the GREAT PRINCE"…

"Prince[8269]" (*sar*) often designates a heavenly being (Daniel 8:11, 25; 10:13, 21; 12:1). The expression "Prince of the host" is never used to designate a high priest in the Old Testament. However, Joshua 5:14–15 clearly designates the "Prince of the host of Yahweh:"

> "And he said, Nay; but *as* captain of the host of the LORD am I now come. And Joshua fell on his face to the earth, and did worship, and said unto him, What saith my lord unto his servant? And the captain of the LORD'S host said unto Joshua, Loose thy shoe from off thy foot; for the place whereon thou standest *is* holy. And Joshua did so."

In Daniel 12:1 Michael is "the Great Prince," and in Jude 9 Michael is identified with Christ. In other words, the "Great Prince" is none other than Jesus Christ.

## DAN. 12:1…"STAND UP"…

"Stand up" signifies the close of probation and that Christ arises to deliver His people. (See, Ellen White, *Great Controversy*, 613, 633, 641, 642, 657).

## DAN. 12:1…"which STANDETH for the children of THY PEOPLE:"…

"Standeth for" Heb. *hab 'omed 'al*, "who stands over," that is, in protection.

## DAN. 12:1…"and there shall be a TIME of TROUBLE such as never was since there was a nation *even* to that same time:"…

> "The world has rejected His mercy, despised His love, and trampled upon His law. The wicked have passed the boundary of their probation; the Spirit of God, persistently resisted, has been at last withdrawn. Unsheltered by divine grace, they have no protection from the wicked one. Satan will then plunge the inhabitants of the earth into one great, final trouble. As the angels of God cease to hold in check the fierce winds of human passion, all the elements of strife will be let loose. The whole world will

be involved in ruin more terrible than that which came upon Jerusalem of old."[140]


## DAN. 12:1..."and at THAT TIME"...

The time period specified here is during the "time of trouble," the falling of the seven last plagues, the means by which the papacy comes to her end.


## DAN. 12:1..."thy people shall be DELIVERED" ...

God's people are delivered from martyrdom at the commencement of the seven last plagues, but they are not delivered from their oppressors until the commencement of the fifth plague:

> "With shouts of triumph, jeering, and imprecation, throngs of evil men are about to rush upon their prey, when, lo, *a dense blackness, deeper than the darkness of the night, falls upon the earth*. Then a rainbow, shining with the glory from the throne of God, spans the heavens and seems to encircle each praying company. The angry multitudes are suddenly arrested. Their mocking cries die away. The objects of their murderous rage are forgotten. With fearful forebodings they gaze upon the symbol of God's covenant and long to be shielded from its overpowering brightness.
>
> By the people of God a voice, clear and melodious, is heard, saying, "Look up," and lifting their eyes to the heavens, they behold the bow of promise. The black, angry clouds that covered the firmament are parted, and like Stephen they look up steadfastly into heaven and see the glory of God and the Son of man seated upon His throne. In His divine form they discern the marks of His humiliation; and from His lips they hear the request presented before His Father and the holy angels: "I will that they also, whom Thou hast given Me, be with Me where I am." John 17:24. Again a voice, musical and triumphant, is heard, saying: "They come! they come! holy, harmless, and undefiled. They have kept the word of My patience; they shall walk among the angels;" and the pale, quivering lips of those who have held fast their faith *utter a shout of victory*. It is at *midnight that God manifests His power for the deliverance of His people*. The sun appears, shining in its strength. Signs and

---

140 Ellen White, *Great Controversy,* 614.

wonders follow in quick succession. The wicked look with terror and amazement upon the scene, *while the righteous behold with solemn joy the tokens of their deliverance*. Everything in nature seems turned out of its course."[141]

This deliverance will be followed very shortly by the deliverance of those in the special resurrection in Dan. 12:2 and then to be followed by the first or general resurrection with all then receiving the touch of immortality.

### DAN. 12:1…"EVERY ONE that shall be found written in THE BOOK."

This "book" is the book of life:

> Dan. 7:10 "A fiery stream issued and came forth from before him: thousand thousands ministered unto him, and ten thousand times ten thousand stood before him: the judgment was set, and the books were opened."

> Rev. 13:8 "And all that dwell upon the earth shall worship him, whose names are not written in the book of life of the Lamb slain from the foundation of the world."

> Rev. 20:15 "And whosoever was not found written in the book of life was cast into the lake of fire."

> Rev. 21:27 "And there shall in no wise enter into it any thing that defileth, neither *whatsoever* worketh abomination, or *maketh* a lie: but they which are written in the Lamb's book of life."

Jesus invites "every one" for no man or woman is denied the promise of God:

> Rev. 22:17 "And the Spirit and the bride say, Come. And let him that heareth say, Come. And let him that is athirst come. And whosoever will, let him take the water of life freely."

To share the eternal happiness that awaits those who no longer are to be tested and tried in the furnace of affliction ever again

---

141 Ellen White, *Great Controversy*, 635–6.

is but for only a moment when compared to eternity, my friend. Jesus opens wide the pearly gates to everyone who will pick up his or her cross and follow Him wherever He may take us for this short probationary period. Let us forever keep in view the love that has been so abundantly displayed for us by Christ for fallen humanity and the reward of the faithful, encouraging all men in the fight of faith. May the world see that love displayed in us, even under the most forbidding circumstances is my sincere prayer:

"Before the ransomed throng is the Holy City. Jesus opens wide the pearly gates, and the nations that have kept the truth enter in. There they behold the Paradise of God, the home of Adam in his innocency. Then that voice, richer than any music that ever fell on mortal ear, is heard, saying: "Your conflict is ended." "Come, ye blessed of My Father, inherit the kingdom prepared for you from the foundation of the world."[142]

---

142 Ellen White, *Great Controversy*, 646.

# APPENDIX I

## Our Explicate Counsel in Proclaiming the Second and Third Angels' Messages under the Coming Crisis.

We previously witnessed that when the King of the North (the papacy) commences her final onslaught against God's Church, she will first focus her energies on undermining religious liberty. That will culminate in the union of church and state in America, which will manifest itself in a legislated national Sunday law. That, in turn, will fully resurrect persecution. When does this event take place? What precipitates this open onslaught which brings about a union of church and state? We are not told, but the issue will be religious liberty—freedom of conscience. Once this event is seen to be taking place, we have clear counsel as to what is to be our work and response, to preserve the work of religious liberty:

"A season of great trial is before us. It becomes us now to use all our capabilities and gifts in advancing the work of God. The powers the Lord has given us are to be used to build up, not to tear down. Those who are ignorantly deceived are not to remain in this condition. The Lord says to His messengers: Go to them and declare unto them what I have said, whether they will hear, or whether they will forbear.

The time is right upon us when persecution will come to those who proclaim the truth. The outlook is not flattering; but, notwithstanding this, let us not give up our efforts to save those ready to perish, for whose ransom the Prince of heaven offered up His precious life. When one means fails, try another. Our efforts must not be dead and lifeless. As long as life is spared, let us work for God. In all ages of the church God's appointed messengers have exposed themselves to reproach and persecution for the truth's sake. But wherever God's people may be forced to go, even though, like the beloved disciple, they are banished to desert islands, Christ will know where they are and will strengthen and bless them, filling them with peace and joy.

Soon there is to be trouble all over the world. It becomes everyone to seek to know God. We have no time to delay."[143]

It is in this crisis of religious liberty that God's people will fully present the second angel's message to the world. When the sins of Rome and the apostate churches are opened before all, and:

> "The fearful results of enforcing the observances of the church by civil authority" are chronicled, persecution will then most certainly rear her ugly head.[144]

This will pave the way for the third angel's message to go forth wtih great power:

> "….As the question of enforcing Sunday observance is [being] widely agitated, the event so long doubted and disbelieved is *seen* to be *approaching*, and the third message will produce an effect which it could not have had before."[145]

It was this very issue of religious liberty that Ellen White said was the commencement of the crisis in 1888 that, had it been permitted to follow through to its conclusion, would have brought on the national Sunday law in America back then:

> "The crisis is now upon us. The battle is to be waged between the Christianity of the Bible and the Christianity of human tradition. Is there not a criminal neglect in our present sleepy condition? There must be a decided advance movement among us. We must show to the world that we recognize, in the events that are now taking place in connection with the National Reform movement, the fulfillment of prophecy. That which we have, for the last thirty or forty years, proclaimed would come, is now here; and the trumpet of every watchman upon the walls of Zion should raise the alarm."[146]

> "It is our duty to do all in our power to avert the threatened danger. We should endeavor to disarm prejudice by placing ourselves in a proper light before the people. We should

143 Ellen White, *Testimonies for the Church,* 9:227–8.

144 Ellen White, *Great Controversy,* 606.

145 Ellen White, *Great Controversy,* 606.

146 *Review and Herald,* January 1, 1889.

bring before them the real question at issue, thus interposing the most effectual protest against measures to restrict liberty of conscience."[147]

God, faced with an unready church and perhaps for other reasons known only to Himself, did not allow the event to come to fruition in 1888. But the same crisis will come again, and He, in His timing, will permit it to come to its evil climax. What are the implications for a commandment-keeping church? What is to be her response to the crisis? It is a crisis of the same nature that Seventh-day Adventists will be called to meet once again by presenting the present truth for this time as it is found in the three angels' messages—a work that, according to, Ellen White, *The Review and Herald*, October 31, 1899, was to be repeated during the final crisis:

> "In a special sense Seventh-day Adventists have been set in the world as watchmen and light bearers. To them has been entrusted the last warning for a perishing world. On them is shining wonderful light from the word of God. They have been given a work of the most solemn import—the proclamation of the first, second, and third angels' messages. There is no other work of so great importance. They are to allow nothing else to absorb their attention. The most solemn truths ever entrusted to mortals have been given us to proclaim to the world. The proclamation of these truths is to be our work. The world is to be warned, and God's people are to be true to the trust committed to them."[148]

The second angel's message is to be repeated in this satanically-inspired showdown, but this time, in all its fullness. In order to do so, it is imperative that God's last-day remnant comprehend the core issues:

> "And there followed another angel, saying, Babylon is fallen, is fallen, that great city, because she made all nations drink of the wine of the wrath of her fornication." Revelation 14:8.

> "The second angel's message of Revelation 14 was first preached in the summer of 1844, and it then had a more direct

---

147 Ellen White, *Testimonies for the Church,* 5:452.

148 Ellen White, *Testimonies for the Church,* 9:19.

application to the churches of the United States, where the warning of the judgment had been most widely proclaimed and most generally rejected, and where the declension in the churches had been most rapid. *But the message of the second angel did not reach its complete fulfillment in 1844.* The churches *then* experienced a *moral fall*, in consequence of their refusal of the light of the advent message; *but that fall was not complete.* As they have continued to reject the special truths for this time they have fallen lower and lower. Not yet, however, can it be said that 'Babylon is fallen,...because she made all nations drink of the wine of the wrath of her fornication.' *She has not yet made [compelled] all nations do this....The change is a progressive one, and the perfect fulfillment of Revelation 14:8 is yet future.*"[149]

"When the churches spurned the counsel of God by rejecting the Advent message, the Lord rejected them. The first angel was followed by a second, proclaiming, 'Babylon is fallen, is fallen, that great city, because she made all nations drink of the wine of the wrath of her fornication.' [Revelation 14:8] This message was understood by Adventists to be an announcement of the moral fall of the churches in consequence of their rejection of the first message. The proclamation, 'Babylon is fallen,' was given in the summer of 1844, and as the result, about fifty thousand withdrew from these churches. The term Babylon, derived from Babel, and signifying confusion, is applied in Scripture to the various forms of false or apostate religion. But the message announcing the fall of Babylon must apply to some religious body that was once pure, and has become corrupt. It cannot be the Romish Church which is here meant; for that church has been in a fallen condition for many centuries. But how appropriate the figure as applied to the Protestant churches."[150]

It was in the summer of 1844 when the Protestant churches, having rejected the Advent message, resorted to *force* by disfellowshiping and removing their members. It was then that they sealed their moral fall. As a consequence, about fifty thousand who accepted the first angel's message and the doctrine of the second coming were compelled to withdraw from those churches.

---

149 Ellen White, *Great Controversy*, 389–90.

150 Ellen White, *Spirit of Prophecy*, 4:232–3.

The rejection of the first angel's message and resultant expulsion from the Protestant churches of those whose consciences received it was but the first step in a three-stage fall of Babylon. The daughters of Babylon will but follow the behavior pattern of their mother church. In the 1840s came the rejection stage when light was refused. When the image of the beast shall be set up and a Sunday law legislated, that will be the replacement stage. Enforcement of that law will be the final step, which will fully reveal the principles and consequences of satanic rule. Our purpose in this study is to fully develop the central issue in the fall of Babylon—the topic of the second angel's message: the issue of religious liberty—the right to worship and obey God as each believes, or the abridgment of that right through some use of force or superior power to compel otherwise.

In 1888 Ellen White compared the treatment she was then receiving from the brethren to the experience of her family four decades earlier:

> "I told them of the hard position I was placed in, to stand, as it were, alone and be compelled to reprove the wrong spirit that was a controlling power at that meeting. The suspicion and jealousy, the evil surmisings, the resistance of the Spirit of God that was appealing to them, were more after the order in which the Reformers had been treated. It was the very order in which the church had treated my father's family and eight of us—the entire family living in Portland, Maine, were excluded from the church because we favored the message proclaimed by William Miller."[151]

This spirit of intolerance—of religious bigotry on the part of the majority—is addressed in explicit terms and requires our attention:

> "Those who endeavor to obey all the commandments of God will be opposed and derided. They can stand only in God. In order to endure the trial before them, they must understand the will of God as revealed in His word; they can honor Him only as they have a right conception of His character, government, and purposes, and act in accordance with them. None but

---

151 Ellen White, *Manuscript Releases,* 16:213.

those who have fortified the mind with the truths of the Bible will stand through the last great conflict."[152]

In order to honor our Father regardless of our trials and to ultimately stand in His presence, we must have "a right conception of His *character, government* and *purposes,* and act in accordance with them." We believe His *character* and *purposes* are clearly understood by all, but what does Inspiration mean by His *government?* Isaiah, speaking of Christ, said:

> "For unto us a child is born, unto us a son is given: and the government shall be upon his shoulder: and his name shall be called Wonderful, Counsellor, The mighty God, The everlasting Father, The Prince of Peace. Of the increase of his government and peace there shall be no end, upon the throne of David, and upon his kingdom, to order it, and to establish it with judgment and with justice from henceforth even for ever. The zeal of the LORD of hosts will perform this." Isaiah 9:6–7.

Christ came to show us the Father; that would include His character and principles of government. If we are at last to find a place among the heavenly throng, we will have first developed His character and accepted those principles here, living daily in accord with them, for we have been informed that it is "the highest crime to rebel against the government of God." *Spirit of Prophecy,* 1:22. Fortunately, we are not left to flounder in speculation as to what constitutes the government of God. Inspiration has minutely defined what that government is:

> 1. "The law of *love* being the foundation of the government of God...."[153]

> 2. "*Justice* and *mercy* are the foundation of the law and government of God."[154]

> 3. "The law of God is the foundation of his Government in Heaven and in earth."[155]

---

152  Ellen White, *Great Controversy,* 593–4.

153  Ellen White, *Great Controversy,* 493.

154  Ibid., 503.

155  Ellen White, *Signs of the Times,* March 30, 1888.

"Christ would have all understand the events of his second appearing. The judgment scene will take place in the presence of all the worlds; for in this judgment the government of God will be vindicated, and *his law* will stand forth as 'holy, and just, and good.' Then every case will be decided, and sentence will be passed upon all. Sin will not then appear attractive, but will be seen in all its hideous magnitude. All will see the relation in which they stand to God and to one another."[156]

4. "The government of God is not, as Satan would make it appear, founded upon a blind submission, an unreasoning control. It appeals to the intellect and the conscience. 'Come now, and let us reason together,' is the Creator's invitation to the beings He has made. Isaiah 1:18. *God does not force the will of His creatures. He cannot accept an homage that is not willingly and intelligently given.* He desires that all the inhabitants of the universe shall be convinced of His justice in the final overthrow of rebellion and the eradication of sin. He purposes that the real nature and direful effects of sin shall be clearly manifested to the end that all may be assured of the wisdom and justice of the divine government."[157]

"The perfectly saved will be perfectly free. Throughout eternity they will do just what they please, because they please to do just what makes liberty and joy possible. Now, as to the relation of the state to the conscience of man. Christ found men enslaved to kings and to priests...After having made men free to sin, that the internal principle of love might work itself out in outward acts of righteousness unhindered by force,..."[158]

Hence we see that the government of God consists of love, justice and mercy; His law; and freedom of choice. Divinely-ordained free will, acknowledged in the concept of religious liberty, is the very essence of the second angel's message of Revelation, 14:8, which verse reveals that force and the compelling of the conscience is contrary to the government of God.

A contributor to *The Southern Watchman* wrote:

---

156 Ellen White, *Review and Herald,* September 20, 1898.

157 Ellen White, *Bible Training School*, December 1, 1908.

158 Ellen White, *The Watchman*, May 1, 1906.

"All slavery, physical, moral, and intellectual, comes from breaking that law. Liberty is found only in obedience to it....His will becomes ours, and with Christ we delight to do His will, because His law is in our hearts. Here is perfect liberty. The perfectly saved will be perfectly free. Throughout eternity they will do just what they please, because they please to do just what makes liberty and joy possible. Now, as to the relation of the state to the conscience of man. Christ found men enslaved to kings and to priests....After having made men free to [from] sin, that the internal principle of love might work itself out in outward acts of righteousness unhindered by force,...has God given to any human authority the right to take away that freedom, and so thwart His plans? He has commanded all men to worship Him and obey His precepts, and this command applies to each individual personally; but has He ever commanded any man or set of men to compel others to worship Him, or to act even outwardly as if they worshiped Him? To ask these questions is to answer them emphatically in the negative...

When Peter, as a member of the Christian church, sought to defend the truth by the sword, Jesus, pointing to His Father as the Church's only source of power, said, 'Put up again thy sword into its place; for all they that take the sword [i.e., in religious matters] shall perish with the sword.' [Mat. 26:52] The tares are to be allowed to grow with the wheat until the harvest. Then God will send forth His angels to gather out the tares and burn them. No human effort of arbitrary force can be used in rooting them out, lest in the act the wheat shall be rooted also. [Mat. 13:30] Again Jesus said, 'My kingdom is not of this world, if my kingdom were of this world, then would my servants fight.' [Jn. 18:36] Every civil law has the power of the sword back of it. If it is right to make law, then it is right to enforce it. In denying to the church the power of the sword, Jesus therefore forbade the church to ask the state for laws enforcing religious beliefs and observances. Paul understood this when he said, 'The weapons of our warfare are not carnal, but mighty through God to the pulling down of strongholds.' [2 Cor. 10:4] The early church, strong only in the power of God, triumphed grandly, even over the opposing forces of a false religion, upheld by the state. Only when she allied herself with the state, seeking its aid, did she deny her God, lose her power, and darken the world into a night of a thousand years. The present effort of the church to get the state to enforce the observance of Sunday, and to introduce the teaching of Christianity into state schools, is but a revival of the pagan and papal doctrine of force in religious things, and as such it is antichristian."[159]

The entire world will see the contrast between the principles of the government of God and that of Satan's, and the entire world will choose their allegiance to one side of this issue or the other. They are to be warned, but we must not act independently, for by so doing we will close up our work prematurely and bring on a persecution that we are not yet prepared to meet. Indeed, definitive counsel has been given to God's people of which is of the utmost import. If not followed by all, Inspiration has revealed that the whole body of Adventism will suffer, even from just one reckless individual:

> "The question of religious liberty is very important, and it should be handled with great wisdom and discretion. Unless this is done there is danger that by our own course of action we shall bring upon ourselves a crisis before we are prepared for it."[160]

Mindful of that counsel, we must nevertheless act:

> "We must soon wrestle with the powers of the land, and we have every reason to fear that falsehood will gain the mastery. We shall call upon our churches in the name of the Lord to view this struggle in its true light....This contest is to decide whether the pure gospel shall have the field in our nation, or whether the popery of past ages shall receive the right hand of fellowship from Protestantism, and this power prevail to restrict religious liberty....The message must go broadcast, that those who have been imperceptibly tampering with popery, not knowing what they were doing, may hear...."[161]

Yes, the time is just before us when we will call our church members to action, so that all may hear this heaven-sent warning message to those who wish to restrict religious liberty. In this message heaven still extends the invitation of the gospel in the first angel's message as well as in the second.

---

159 George Fifield, *The Southern Watchman*, May 1, 1906.

160 Ellen White, *Testimonies for Ministers,* 219.

161 Ellen White, *Selected Messages,* 3:385–6.

The hellish principles behind an attempt to control the conscience are rarely touched upon, but the people of God will experience their full impact in the very near future. This is why we have taken a departure here from our scriptural study of Daniel 11:40–45 to look into this much-misunderstood and neglected topic and reveal the first work that heaven has commissioned the people of God to do when the King of the North "enters" into the realm of the church. When we, as a people, fully take in the concepts of religious liberty that are foundational to the government of God, we will have a powerful testimony for the truth that cannot be overthrown. We must understand and proclaim that faith itself demands freedom.

When the conscience is controlled through force, faith ceases to be faith. Love disappears and the motive for obedience then becomes fear. It is only through religious freedom that faith can find its fullest potential and expression. Faith, therefore, has its best protection in religious liberty. In an unrestricted religious environment, where one's faith is not governed by mandatory limitations or coercion, faith is an unlimited and voluntary "choice in action." Faith is free to be expressed in the choices one makes regarding the invitation and, in fact, every aspect of the gospel:

> "And the Spirit and the bride say, Come. And let him that heareth say, Come. And let him that is athirst come. And whosoever will, let him take the water of life freely." Rev. 22:17.

In fact, religious liberty and true faith are mutually dependent upon one another, for whoever endangers or restricts religious liberty threatens or restricts truth itself, for truth is forever unfolding to the one who lives and walks by faith. When the soul is prevented from seeking where it will, when it is demanded that the individual conform to certain religious doctrines or practices, when the mind is subjugated to another human being, no true spiritual growth can occur. The religious experience will be dwarfed or stalled. And with no living experience, there can be no character development, and thus no sanctification. Hence Satan wins.

> "Some will be convicted [by faith] and [by faith] will heed the words spoken to them in love and tenderness. They will acknowledge that the *truth is the very thing they need to set*

*them free* from the slavery of sin and the bondage of worldly principles. There are opened before them themes of thought, fields for action that they had never comprehended."[162]

Only living faith leads to spiritual growth. A formality of religious experience contributes to nothing but an external experience, which is valueless with God. It is faith alone that, above all other considerations, makes men free, because only in free exercise of faith—freedom to believe and follow as suits the heart of each—can man be the free moral agent God created him to be. Paul exemplified that principle in 1 Corinthians 9:19, referring to himself as "free from all men."

> "It is not God's purpose to coerce the will. Man was created a free moral agent. Like the inhabitants of all other worlds, he must be subjected to the test of obedience; but he is never brought into such a position that yielding to evil becomes a matter of necessity."[163]

It is only by a clear understanding of this matter for ourselves that we will properly proclaim the second angel's message, thus fulfilling our divine commission during the final crisis. Therefore, "let every man be fully persuaded in his own mind." Romans 14:5.

> "The exercise of force is contrary to the principles of God's government; He desires only the service of love; and love cannot be commanded; it cannot be won by force or authority. Only by love is love awakened."[164]

The scriptures present clear instruction on the path the church must take in the conflict between tolerance and intolerance:

> "And it came to pass, when the time was come that he should be received up, he stedfastly set his face to go to Jerusalem, And sent messengers before his face: and they went, and entered into a village of the Samaritans, to make ready for him. And they did not receive him, because his face was as though he would go to Jerusalem. And when his disciples James and John saw this, they said, Lord, wilt thou that we command fire to come down from heaven,

---

162 Ellen White, *Medical Ministry,* 244.

163 Ellen White, *Patriarchs and Prophets,* 331–2.

164 Ellen White, *Desire of Ages,* 22.

and consume them, even as Elias did? But he turned, and rebuked them, and said, Ye know not what manner of spirit ye are of. For the Son of man is not come to destroy men's lives, but to save them...." Luke 9:51–6.

It was on the matter of intolerance that the church was sternly rebuked. The disciples were reminded of the power which alone was to govern their lives, namely the Holy Spirit:

> "James and John, Christ's messengers, were greatly annoyed at the insult shown to their Lord [when the Samaritans refused hospitality to Jesus, because his face was set to go to Jerusalem]. They were filled with indignation because He had been so rudely treated by the Samaritans whom He was honoring by His presence. They had recently been with Him on the mount of transfiguration, and had seen Him glorified by God, and honored by Moses and Elijah. This manifest dishonor on the part of the Samaritans, should not, they thought, be passed over without marked punishment.
>
> "Coming to Christ, they reported to Him the words of the people, telling Him that they had even refused to give Him a night's lodging. They thought that a grievous wrong had been done Him, and seeing Mount Carmel in the distance, where Elijah had slain the false prophets, they said, 'Wilt Thou that we command fire to come down from heaven, and consume them, even as Elias did?' They were surprised to see that Jesus was pained by their words, and still more surprised as His rebuke fell upon their ears, '*Ye know not what manner of spirit ye are of.* For the Son of man is not come to destroy men's lives, but to save them.' And He went to another village."[165]

That we are to speak up for the truth is made plain:

> "...What is the duty of the messenger of truth? Shall he conclude that the truth ought not to be presented, since often its only effect is to arouse men to evade or resist its claims? No; he has no more reason for withholding the testimony of God's word, because it excites opposition, than had earlier Reformers....[They] received grace and truth, not for themselves alone, but that, through them, the knowledge of God might enlighten the earth.

---

165 Ellen White, *Desire of Ages,* 487.

Has God given light to His servants in this generation? Then they should let it shine forth to the world."[166]

But *how* we are to speak up for the truth is also made plain:

"It is no part of Christ's mission to compel men to receive Him. It is Satan, and men actuated by his spirit, that seek to compel the conscience. Under a pretense of zeal for righteousness, men who are confederate with evil angels bring suffering upon their fellow men, in order to convert them to their ideas of religion; but Christ is ever showing mercy, ever seeking to win by the revealing of His love.

"He can admit no rival in the soul, nor accept of partial service; but He desires only voluntary service, the willing surrender of the heart under the constraint of love. There can be no more conclusive evidence that we possess the spirit of Satan than the disposition to hurt and destroy those who do not appreciate our work, or who act contrary to our ideas. Every human being, in body, soul, and spirit, is the property of God. Christ died to redeem all. Nothing can be more offensive to God than for men, through religious bigotry, to bring suffering upon those who are the purchase of the Saviour's blood."[167]

Clearly, then, we can see that those who are in harmony with the government of God will never coerce the will of another to achieve their ends. God's way is to "draw all men unto" Himself, to "receive" us when we *choose* to "turn" and "come unto" Him. His way allows only for freedom of choice.

On the other hand, those who have enlisted under the government of Satan have no scruples to bring suffering upon those whom they cannot control:

"Compelling power is found only under Satan's government." Ellen White, *Desire of Ages*, 759. Therefore, his subjects are ever ready to use force in any or all its various forms to compel others to accept their bigoted ideas of religion. This is why Inspiration says, "Force is the last resort of every false religion."[168]

---

166 Ellen White, *Great Controversy*, 459.

167 Ellen White, *Desire of Ages,* 487–8.

168 Ellen White, *SDA Bible Commentary,* 7:976.

Luther himself, who had firsthand experience with this spirit of intolerance, said, "Even this is an evil zeal, not from God but from the devil."[169]

We must always remember during this trying hour that any form of retaliation by means and methods of a carnal nature is to make shipwreck of faith, for vengeance is the sole right of God alone. No carnal instruments should be on hand or taken in hand by the people of God, lest they fall into temptation:

> "The truth should be presented with divine tact, gentleness, and tenderness. It should come from a heart that has been softened and made sympathetic. We need to have close communion with God, lest self rise up, as it did in Jehu, and we pour forth a torrent of words that are unbefitting....
>
> "Make no reference to what opponents say, but let the truth alone be advanced....
>
> "As trials thicken around us, both separation and unity will be seen in our ranks. Some who are now ready to take up weapons of warfare will in times of real peril make it manifest that they have not built upon the solid rock; they will yield to temptation. Those who have had great light and precious privileges, but have not improved them, will, under one pretext or another, go out from us."[170]

> "'Whereunto,' asked Christ, 'shall we liken the kingdom of God? or with what comparison shall we compare it?' Mark 4:30. He could not employ the kingdoms of the world as a similitude. In society He found nothing with which to compare it. Earthly kingdoms rule by the ascendancy of physical power; but from Christ's kingdom every carnal weapon, every instrument of coercion, is banished."[171]

> "This is the instruction and mandate for our church, whether we be laity, independent, conference, academic, or any other Christian community. If we are to endure the trial before us, we must first have "a right conception of His *character*, *government*, and *purposes*, and then act in accordance with them."[172]

---

169 Luther, *Sermon on Luke 9:51*, (1537); Weimar ed., t. 45, p. 407.

170 Ellen White, *Testimonies for the Church,* 6:400.

171 Ellen White, *Acts of the Apostles,* 12.

172 Ellen White, *Great Controversy,* 593.

We will then be equipped in principle to take the second angel's message to the world and receive our fuller instruction:

> "In cases where we are brought before the courts, we are to give up our rights unless it brings us in collision with God. It is not our rights we are pleading for, but God's right to our service."[173]

Here is far-seeing counsel. Many who will be opposed to the One World Order have no connection to Christ. They will fight for their rights. Adventists, though, are to have nothing to do with and nothing to say about our rights which are being taken away—unless their revocation interferes with God's right to our worship and service. This will keep us out of unnecessary persecution and disassociate us from others who most likely will use carnal methods in order to be heard or seen in their protest. However, when the retraction of our civil rights does cross the bridge into a denial of religious liberty, we have our explicit instruction.

Divine counsel was given in the late 1880s when a bill voiding religious liberty was presented for Congressional consideration. That counsel comes to us, as well, for a time when the same cause will produce the same result:

> "While the Protestant world is, by her attitude, *making concessions to Rome*, we should arouse to comprehend the situation, and view the contest before us in its true bearings. While men have slept, Satan has been stealthily sowing the tares. Let the watchmen *now* lift up their voice like a trumpet, and give the message which is present truth for this time. Let them know where we are in prophetic history, that the spirit of true Protestantism may awaken all the world to a sense of the value of the privileges of religious liberty so long enjoyed."[174]

What shall be the result if God's people do not respond to proclaim the second angel's message?:

> "Let none sit in calm expectation of the evil, comforting themselves with the belief that this work must go on because prophecy has foretold it, and that the Lord will shelter His

---

173 Ellen White, *Manuscript Releases,* 5:69.

174 Ellen White, *Review and Herald,* January 1, 1889.

people. We are not doing the will of God if we sit in quietude, doing nothing to preserve liberty of conscience....If our people continue in the listless attitude in which they have been, *God cannot pour upon them His Spirit.*"[175]

Imagine if you can, at the very commencement of the crisis, the danger of entering into the battle against the host of evil without the aid of the Holy Spirit. God forbid. Therefore, our very response and attitude to this call carries eternal consequences. Let us continue, then, with our instruction:

"By some of our brethren many things have been spoken and written that are interpreted as expressing antagonism to government and law. It is a mistake thus to lay ourselves open to misunderstanding. It is not wise to find fault continually with what is done by the rulers of government. It is not our work to attack individuals or institutions. We should exercise great care lest we be understood as putting ourselves in opposition to the civil authorities. It is true that our warfare is aggressive, but our weapons are to be those found in a plain 'Thus saith the Lord.' Our work is to prepare a people to stand in the great day of God. We should not be turned aside to lines that will encourage controversy or arouse antagonism in those not of our faith.

"We should not work in a manner that will mark us out as seeming to advocate treason. We should weed out from our writings and utterances every expression that, taken by itself, could be so misrepresented as to make it appear antagonistic to law and order. Everything should be carefully considered, lest we place ourselves on record as encouraging disloyalty to our country and its laws. We are not required to defy authorities. There will come a time when, because of our advocacy of Bible truth, we shall be treated as traitors; but let not this time be hastened by unadvised movements that stir up animosity and strife.

"The time will come when unguarded expressions of a denunciatory character, that have been carelessly spoken or written by our brethren, will be used by our enemies to condemn us. These will not be used merely to condemn those who made the statements, but will be charged upon the whole body of Adventists. Our accusers will say that on such and such a day one of our responsible men said thus and so against the administration of the laws of this government. Many will be astonished to see how many things have been cherished and remembered that

---

175 Ellen White, *Testimonies for the Church,* 7:713–4.

will give point to the arguments of our adversaries. Many will be surprised to hear their own words strained into a meaning that they did not intend them to have. Then let our workers be careful to speak guardedly at all times and under all circumstances. Let all beware lest by reckless expressions they bring on a time of trouble before the great crisis which is to try men's souls. The less we make direct charges against authorities and powers, the greater work we shall be able to accomplish, both in America and in foreign countries....

"The workers must be kept by the power of God through faith unto salvation. They must have divine wisdom, that nothing may be uttered which would stir up men to close our way....We need to present the truth in its simplicity, to advocate practical godliness; and we should do this in the spirit of Christ. The manifestation of such a spirit will have the best influence upon our own souls, and it will have a convincing power upon others....

"Stormy times will come rapidly enough upon us, and we should take no course of our own that will hasten them....

"If we wish men to be convinced that the truth we believe sanctifies the soul and transforms the character, let us not be continually charging them with vehement accusations. In this way we shall force them to the conclusion that the doctrine we profess cannot be the Christian doctrine, since it does not make us kind, courteous, and respectful. Christianity is not manifested in pugilistic accusations and condemnation.

"Many of our people are in danger of trying to exercise a controlling power upon others and of bringing oppression upon their fellow men. There is danger that those who are entrusted with responsibilities will acknowledge but one power, the power of an unsanctified will. Some have exercised this power unscrupulously and have caused great discomfiture to those whom the Lord is using. One of the greatest curses in our world (and it is seen in churches and in society everywhere) is the love of supremacy. Men become absorbed in seeking to secure power and popularity. This spirit has manifested itself in the ranks of Sabbathkeepers, to our grief and shame. But spiritual success comes only to those who have learned meekness and lowliness in the school of Christ.

"We should remember that the world will judge us by what we appear to be. Let those who are seeking to represent Christ be careful not to exhibit inconsistent features of character. Before we come fully to the front, let us see to it that the Holy Spirit is poured upon us from on high. When this is the case, we shall give a decided message, but it will be of a far less condemnatory character than that which some have been giving; and all who believe will be far more earnest for the salvation of our opponents. Let God have the matter of condemning authorities and governments wholly in His own keeping. In meekness and love let us as faithful sentinels defend the principles of truth as it is in Jesus."[176]

"It is time for God's people to work as never before....If they do nothing to disabuse the minds of the people, and through ignorance of the truth our legislatures should abjure the principles of Protestantism, and give countenance and support to the Roman fallacy, the spurious sabbath, God will hold his people who have had great light, responsible for their lack of diligence and faithfulness. But if the subject of religious legislation is judiciously and intelligently laid before the people, and they see that through Sunday enforcement the Roman apostasy would be re-enacted by the Christian world, and that the tyranny of past ages would be repeated, *then whatever comes, we shall have done our duty*."[177]

We will briefly review our sacred obligation, as the church of God, to give the law of God the prominence that is needful as the culmination of human history approaches in the impending abrogation of that law. Through us, God intends that the people of the world be given a final opportunity to contrast the government of God with the oppressive rule and government of Satan, through his human agents. With those objectives in mind, we now begin:

"And the third angel followed them, saying with a loud voice, If any man worship the beast and his image, and receive his mark in his forehead, or in his hand, The same shall drink of the wine of the wrath of God, which is poured out without mixture into the cup of his indignation; and he shall be tormented with fire and brimstone in the presence of the holy angels, and in the presence of the Lamb: And the smoke of their torment ascendeth up for ever and ever: and they have no rest day nor night, who worship the beast and his image, and whosoever receiveth the mark of his name. Here is the patience of the saints:

---

176 Ellen White, *Testimonies for the Church,* 6:394–7.

177 Ellen White, *Review and Herald*, December 24, 1889.

here [are] they that keep the commandments of God, and the faith of Jesus." Rev. 14:9–12.

However, before these awful judgments descend upon humanity, God in mercy will first send forth His consecrated laborers to sound the trumpet of alarm:

> "The Lord God of heaven will not send upon the world His judgments for disobedience and transgression until He has sent His watchmen to give the warning. He will not close up the period of probation until the message shall be more distinctly proclaimed. The law of God is to be magnified; its claims must be presented in their true, sacred character, that the people may be brought to decide for or against the truth. Yet the work will be cut short in righteousness. The message of Christ's righteousness is to sound from one end of the earth to the other to prepare the way of the Lord. This is the glory of God, which closes the work of the third angel. There is no work in our world so great, so sacred, and so glorious, no work that God honors so much, as this gospel work. The message presented at this time is the last message of mercy for a fallen world."[178]

Many, however, will be led to reject the Lord's merciful call. Ellen White reveals the intent of the clergy and their united effort to obtain public consensus:

> "If the people can be led to favor a Sunday law, then the clergy intend to exert their united influence to obtain a religious amendment to the Constitution, and compel the nation to keep Sunday."[179]

Inspiration tells us that intention will meet with success. Compulsory Sunday worship in direct opposition to the fourth commandment (the seventh-day Sabbath) will be legislated into power. The fires of persecution will be rekindled. With the image to the beast thus to be set up, the last invitation of salvation will be extended to a perishing world. Now is sounded the command:

---

178 Ellen White, *Testimonies for the Church,* 6:19.

179 Ellen White, *Review and Herald,* December 24, 1889.

"He commands His servants to present the last invitation of mercy to the world. They cannot remain silent, except at the peril of their souls."[180]

As it was regarding the second angel's message, so it will be likewise if one remains silent during this critical period of the third angel's message. It will be at the peril of his own soul. But God's true people must and will press on, heedless of personal consequences:

"Let not the commandment-keeping people of God be silent at this time, as though we gracefully accepted the situation. There is the prospect before us, of waging a continuous war, at the risk of imprisonment, of losing property and even life itself, to defend the law of God, which is being made void by the laws of men. This Bible text will be quoted to us, 'Let every soul be subject unto the higher powers....The powers that be are ordained of God.'"[181]

The argument will be pressed upon us that obedience to the nation's Sunday law is mandated by God, based on the verse just quoted. The instruction to meet that argument was given to us over a century ago:

"The question is asked, Shall we not obey the powers that be?—Yes, when they are in harmony with the higher powers that be."[182]

The principle is straightforward. Heaven has given the state a line to which it can go and no more. It has also given to the church a limit to which she may extend, and no further. Those parameters can be found in Romans 13. While Romans 13 deserves a study of its own, suffice it to be said with just the following. The external, physical acts referred to in the last six commandments, while reflecting man's divinely appointed duty to man, are also under state oversight for temporal enforcement. However, matters of the heart and conscience, delineated on the first table of the Law, are solely between man and God. When religious authorities

---

180  Ellen White, *Great Controversy,* 609.

181  Ellen White, *Review and Herald,* January 1, 1889.

182  Ellen White, *Review and Herald,* April 15, 1890.

presume to intrude upon the internal applications of the first four commandments, and to require an external expression of mental acquiescence, and when the state endeavors to penalize those who don't comply, then religious freedom will have been abridged and humanity must recognize the law of a higher power at whatever the cost it may inflict upon themselves:

> "The people of God will recognize human government as an ordinance of divine appointment and will teach obedience to it as a sacred duty within its legitimate sphere. But when its claims conflict with the claims of God, the word of God must be recognized as above all human legislation. 'Thus saith the Lord' is not to be set aside for Thus saith the church or the state."[183]

The role of the state cannot extend to matters of the heart and conscience:

> "To protect liberty of conscience is the duty of the state, and this is the limit of its authority in matters of religion. Every secular government that attempts to regulate or enforce religious observances by civil authority is sacrificing the very principle for which the evangelical Christian so nobly struggled."[184]

We are referred to an example in God's Word:

> "[King] David's power had been given him by God, but only to be exercised in harmony with the divine law. When he commanded that which was contrary to God's law [the numbering of his kingdom], it became sin to obey. 'The powers that be are ordained of God' (Romans 13:1), but we are not to obey them contrary to God's law. The apostle Paul, writing to the Corinthians, sets forth the principle by which we should be governed. He says, 'Be ye followers of me, even as I also am of Christ.' 1 Corinthians 11:1."[185]

Our instruction from the apostle Peter under the same condition declares:

> "We ought to obey God rather than men." Acts 5:29.

---

183 Ellen White, *Testimonies for the Church,* 6:402.

184 Ellen White, *Great Controversy,* 201.

185 Ellen White, *Patriarchs and Prophets,* 719.

And in another instance:

> "...The prophet [Daniel] boldly yet quietly and humbly declared that no earthly power has a right to interpose between the soul and God."[186]

One cannot misunderstand the counsel:

> "When the laws of men conflict with the word and law of God, we are to obey the latter, whatever the consequences may be."[187]

Cognizant, then, of the great test of faith and character before us, now is the time for us to fortify our minds with God's word and commit to memory those precious promises, for it will be in this hour that many of us will have to stand alone, deprived of our Bibles, to answer for our faith before the legislative assemblies of the land:

> "Put away the foolish reading matter and study the Word of God. Commit its precious promises to memory so that when we shall be deprived of our Bibles we may still be in possession of the Word of God."[188]

> "Urge our people to become familiar with the Word of God. In their study, the students in our schools should commit to memory portions of the Word. The time will come when many will be deprived of the written word. But if this word is printed in the memory, no one can take it from us; and it is a talisman that will meet the worst forms of error and evil."[189]

This is in deep contrast to the mindset of the beast power:

---

186 Ellen White, *Prophets and Kings,* 542.

187 Ellen White, *Testimonies for the Church,* 1:201–2.

188 Ellen White, *Manuscript, 85,* 1909, p. 10; Ellen White, *Manuscript Releases,* 10:298.

189 Ellen White, *Manuscript Releases,* 20:64.

"The Catholic system with the splendid organization of its living magisterium is far superior to the Protestant system, *which rests everything on the authority of a book.*"[190]

Having thus condensed the essential parts of instruction for God's people regarding the second and third angels messages, we encourage the reader to pursue these vital concepts in their fullest application, as they have been largely ignored in recent times.

---

190 *The Catholic Encyclopedia*, "Tradition and Living Magisterium" (New York, The Encyclopedia Press, 1913), 8.

# APPENDIX II

## A few Selective quotes from the pen of Ellen White regarding Labor Unions in the End of Time.

Please notice the *italicized* terms found in the following quotes from Ellen White in contrast to the wording of Rev. 13:15–17. The labor unions of the future are to play a significant role in the martyrdom of the saints:

"Rev. 13:15 "And he had power to give life unto the image of the beast, that the image of the beast should both speak, and cause that as many as would not worship the image of the beast should be killed.""

"Rev. 13:16 "And he causeth all, both small and great, rich and poor, free and bond, to receive a mark in their right hand, or in their foreheads:""

"Rev. 13:17 "And that no man might buy or sell, save he that had the mark, or the name of the beast, or the number of his name.""

"And the trade unions will be one of the agencies that will bring upon this earth a time of trouble such as has not been since the world began." *Letter*, 200, 1903, p. 3. (To Elder G. I. Butler, September 10, 1903.) Ellen White, *Manuscript Releases,* 4:88.

"Satanic agencies are becoming more determined in their rebellion against God. The trade unions will be the cause of the most terrible violence that has ever been seen among human beings."[191]

---

191 Ellen White, *Letter*, 99, 1904, p. 3. (To J. E. White and wife, February 23, 1904.)

"In all our great cities there will be a binding up in bundles by the confederacies and unions formed. Man will rule other men and demand much of them. *The lives of those who refuse to unite with these unions, will be in peril.* Everything is being prepared for the last great work to be done by the One mighty to save and mighty to destroy....

The condition of things before the Flood has been presented to me. The same binding up in unions that exists today existed in Noah's day."[192]

"For years I have been given special light that we are not to center our work in the cities. The turmoil and confusion that fill these cities, the conditions brought about by the labor unions and the strikes, would prove a great hindrance to our work. Men are seeking to bring those engaged in the different trades under bondage to certain unions. This is not God's planning, but the planning of a power that we should in no wise acknowledge. God's word is fulfilling; the wicked are binding themselves up in bundles ready to be burned.

We are now to use all our entrusted capabilities in giving the last warning message to the world. In this work we are to preserve our individuality. We are not to unite with secret societies or with trade-unions. We are to stand *free* in God, looking constantly to Christ for instruction. All our movements are to be made with a realization of the importance of the work to be accomplished for God."[193]

"The work of the people of God is to prepare for the events of the future, which will soon come upon them with blinding force. In the world gigantic monopolies will be formed. Men will bind themselves together in unions that will wrap them in the folds of the enemy. A few men will combine to grasp all the means to be obtained in certain lines of business. Trades unions will be formed, and those who refuse to join these unions will be *marked men*...."

"The principles governing the forming of these unions seem innocent, but men have to pledge themselves to serve the interests of these unions, *or else they may have to pay the penalty of refusal with their lives.*

---

192 Ellen White, *Manuscript Releases,* 3:42.

193 Ellen White, *Testimonies for the Church,* 7:84.

These unions are one of the signs of the last days. Men are binding up in bundles ready to be burned. They may be church members, but while they belong to these unions, they cannot possibly keep the commandments of God; *for to belong to these unions means to disregard the entire decalogue.*"

"Thou shalt love the Lord thy God with all thy heart, and with all thy soul, and with all thy strength, and with all thy mind; and thy neighbor as thyself." These words sum up the whole duty of man. They mean the consecration of the whole being, body, soul, and spirit, to God's service. How can men obey these words, and at the same time pledge themselves to support that which deprives their neighbors of freedom of action? And how can men obey these words, and form combinations that *rob the poorer classes* of the advantages which justly belong to them, *preventing them from buying or selling*, except under certain conditions?" How plainly the words of God have predicted this condition of things. John writes, "I beheld another beast coming up out of the earth; and he had two horns like a lamb, and he spake as a dragon....And he causeth all, both small and great, rich and poor, free and bond, to receive a mark in their right hand, or in their foreheads: and that no man might buy or sell, save he that had the mark, or the name of the beast, or the number of his name" (Revelation 13:11–17)."

"The forming of these unions is one of Satan's *last efforts*. God calls upon His people to get out of the cities, isolating themselves from the world. The time will come when they will have to do this. God will care for those who love Him and keep His commandments."[194]

"Those who claim to be the children of God are in no case to bind up with the labor unions that are formed or that shall be formed. This *the Lord forbids. Cannot those who study the prophecies* [plural] *see and understand what is before us*? The transgressors of the law of God have taken sides with their leader, the general of rebellion. He understands how to devise his satanic schemes and through whom to work for the carrying out of them. He is striving to lead every soul to take sides with him, and under the influence of his temptations, thousands are binding themselves up in bundles, ready to be consumed by the fires of the last day. Those who yield to his

---

194 Ellen White, *Manuscript Releases,* 4:74–6. *Letter,* 26, 1903, pp. 2, 3. (To Brother and Sister J. A. Burden, Dec. 10, 1902).

temptation become in their turn tempters, standing among the ablest of his helpers."[195]

---

195 Ellen White, *Manuscript Releases,* 4:78–9. For further study see: Ellen White, *Manuscript Releases*, 4:66–94.

We invite you to view the complete
selection of titles we publish at:

www.TEACHServices.com

or write or email us your praises,
reactions, or thoughts about this
or any other book we publish at:

## TEACH Services, Inc.
P U B L I S H I N G
*www.TEACHServices.com*
P.O. Box 954
Ringgold, GA 30736

info@TEACHServices.com

Finally, if you are interested in seeing
your own book in print, please contact us at

publishing@teachservices.com.

We would be happy to review your manuscript for free.

www.ingramcontent.com/pod-product-compliance
Lightning Source LLC
Chambersburg PA
CBHW060545100426
42742CB00013B/2452